Against the World For the World

D1260677

Against the World For the World

THE HARTFORD APPEAL AND THE FUTURE OF AMERICAN RELIGION

edited by PETER L. BERGER
and RICHARD JOHN NEUHAUS

A Crossroad Book
THE SEABURY PRESS · NEW YORK

The Seabury Press
815 Second Avenue
New York, N.Y. 10017

Copyright © 1976 by Peter L. Berger and Richard John Neuhaus. All rights reserved.
No part of this book may be reproduced, stored in a retrieval system, or transmitted,
in any form or by any means, electronic, mechanical, photocopying, recording or
otherwise, without the written permission of The Seabury Press.

Printed in the United States of America

Library of Congress Cataloging in Publication Data

Main entry under title:

Against the world for the world.

  "A Crossroad book."
  1. Appeal for theological affirmation. 2. United States—
Religion—1945–   —Congresses. 3. Christianity—20th century—
Congresses. I. Berger, Peter L. II. Neuhaus, Richard John. III.
Appeal for theological affirmation. 1975
BR526.A33   209'.73   75–42142
ISBN 0–8164–0286–8
ISBN 0–8164–2121–8 pbk.

Contents

A Word to The Reader

The Hartford Appeal of January 1975 has been characterized as, among other things, a frivolous caper, a needed assertion of the obvious, and the portent of a new reformation. Others will judge for themselves whatever may be the significance of Hartford. We can only say what we intended by the Appeal and what we hope it might mean for the future of religion in America. That is the purpose of this book.

The authors of the essays in this volume speak for themselves. In this respect the volume continues the spirit of Hartford itself—a totally unauthorized gathering of men and women around shared concerns. Each Hartford participant takes the institutional churches seriously and most are very much involved in more formal theological discussions. Hartford is a different kind of experiment in the doing of ecumenical theology. It is intended not to replace but to complement other and more official ways in which that task is pursued.

A brief word is in order about the background of the Appeal. It began in Brooklyn in the winter of 1974. After many years of discussing together the state of American religion, the editors ventured one evening to put in writing the "pervasive, false and debilitating" notions which they believed were undermining contemporary Christianity and its influence in society. The evening's somewhat whimsical intellectual exercise produced a number of themes and counterthemes which we thought might possibly be of wider interest.

At first we circulated our draft among two dozen or more theologians and religious thinkers of diverse viewpoints, asking for their comments. Eventually many more people were to become involved. In any case, we were not prepared for the vigorous and, for the most part, enthusiastic response. From all sides came the encouragement to arrange a meeting to discuss the issues posed by the draft and, possibly, to issue some kind of public statement.

The participants met in Hartford in late January of the next year and, after three days of the most intensive cooperation and debate, reworked the original draft, achieving unanimous agreement on what then became the Hartford Appeal for Theological Affirmation. The purpose was not to develop a new ecumenical creed. Given the diversity of the group involved, that would likely have been impossible. We did not intend to say all we believed, but merely what we believe about the current state of religious thought in America and what we think is required if the Church is "to address with clarity and courage the urgent tasks to which God calls it in the world."

The signers of the Appeal are those who participated in the process that produced it. A few signers, as noted, were not able to attend the January meeting but had been involved in preliminary stages of the enterprise. No additional signatures have been solicited. The Appeal is not intended as a formal petition or as a manifesto of some new party but simply as a point of reference for continuing discussion. We are well aware that the participants are not entirely representative of every group or category of persons comprising American Christianity. That too is part of being an unauthorized event. Certainly there are many, many more people who could have made significant contributions in formulating the Appeal. Obviously it was necessary to keep the group to a workable size and at some point the participants simply had to go ahead with what they had. In short, Hartford was, as they used to say, a happening. It is marked by a very high degree of the serendipitous.

The response to date has far exceeded the expectations of the participants. Both here and elsewhere, notably in Europe, the Appeal has been greeted by acclaim, ridicule, anger, and, especially among laypeople, an enormous sense of relief that "somebody finally said what needed to be said." Whatever may or may not be the merits of the Appeal, the response to it unquestionably says something important about the current state of religion.

An appeal such as this must of necessity be brief. Perhaps this one was too brief. Be that as it may, the debate surrounding the Hartford Appeal is frequently marked by misunderstandings and ambiguities. Therefore the participants came together again in September of 1975 in order to clarify and elaborate the intention of the Appeal. The essays prepared for and discussed at that meeting make up this book. Thus, while the authors speak for themselves, they do so in conversation with the other participants. The result, we believe, accurately reflects the range and diversity of views that shaped the Hartford Appeal.

Hartford is not designed to exclude anyone from theological discourse or to foreclose possibilities. On the contrary, it is a wide-open invitation and, we hope, a useful referent in what must be an energetic and multifarious exchange on the future of religion in our kind of world. To that end we hope this book will be of some modest help.

Finally, we are deeply grateful to James Gettemy and to the Hartford Seminary Foundation of which he is president for making available the funds of the Carew Lectureship for the meetings that produced the Appeal and this book.

Peter L. Berger
Richard John Neuhaus

An Appeal for Theological Affirmation

The renewal of Christian witness and mission requires constant examination of the assumptions shaping the Church's life. Today an apparent loss of a sense of the transcendent is undermining the Church's ability to address with clarity and courage the urgent tasks to which God calls it in the world. This loss is manifest in a number of pervasive themes. Many are superficially attractive, but upon closer examination we find these themes false and debilitating to the Church's life and work. Among such themes are:

Theme 1: *Modern thought is superior to all past forms of understanding reality, and is therefore normative for Christian faith and life.*

In repudiating this theme we are protesting the captivity to the prevailing thought structures not only of the twentieth century but of any historical period. We favor using any helpful means of understanding, ancient or modern, and insist that the Christian proclamation must be related to the idiom of the culture. At the same time, we affirm the need for Christian thought to confront and be confronted by other world views, all of which are necessarily provisional.

Theme 2: *Religious statements are totally independent of reasonable discourse.*

The capitulation to the alleged primacy of modern thought takes two forms: one is the subordination of religious statements to the canons of scientific rationality; the other, equating reason with scientific rationality, would remove religious statements from the realm of reasonable discourse altogether. A religion of pure subjectivity and nonrationality results in treating faith statements as being, at best, statements about the believer. We repudiate both forms of capitulation.

Theme 3: *Religious language refers to human experience and nothing else, God being humanity's noblest creation.*

Religion is also a set of symbols and even of human projections. We repudiate the assumption that it is nothing but that. What is here at stake is nothing less than the reality of God: *We did not invent God; God invented us.*

Theme 4: *Jesus can only be understood in terms of contemporary models of humanity.*

This theme suggests a reversal of "the imitation of Christ"; that is, the image of Jesus is made to reflect cultural and countercultural notions of human excellence. We do not deny that all aspects of humanity are illumined by Jesus. Indeed, it is necessary to the universality of the Christ that he be perceived in relation to the particularities of the believers' world. We do repudiate the captivity to such metaphors, which are necessarily inadequate, relative, transitory, and frequently idolatrous. Jesus, together with the Scriptures and the whole of the Christian tradition, cannot be arbitrarily interpreted without reference to the history of which they are part. The danger is in the attempt to exploit the tradition without taking the tradition seriously.

Theme 5: *All religions are equally valid; the choice among them is not a matter of conviction about truth but only of personal preference or life style.*

We affirm our common humanity. We affirm the importance of exploring and confronting all manifestations of the religious quest and of learning from the riches of other religions. But we repudiate this theme because it flattens diversities and ignores contradictions. In doing so, it not only obscures the meaning of Christian faith, but also fails to respect the integrity of other faiths. Truth matters; therefore differences among religions are deeply significant.

Theme 6: *To realize one's potential and to be true to oneself is the whole meaning of salvation.*

Salvation contains a promise of human fulfillment, but to identify salvation with human fulfillment can trivialize the promise. We affirm that salvation cannot be found apart from God.

Theme 7: *Since what is human is good, evil can adequately be understood as failure to realize potential.*

This theme invites false understanding of the ambivalence of human existence and underestimates the pervasiveness of sin. Paradoxically, by minimizing the enormity of evil, it undermines serious and sustained attacks on particular social or individual evils.

Theme 8: *The sole purpose of worship is to promote individual self-realization and human community.*

Worship promotes individual and communal values, but it is above all a response to the reality of God and arises out of the fundamental need and desire to know, love, and adore God. We worship God because God is to be worshiped.

Theme 9: *Institutions and historical traditions are oppressive and inimical to our being truly human; liberation from*

*them is required for authentic existence and authentic reli-
gion.*

Institutions and traditions are often oppressive. For this
reason they must be subjected to relentless criticism. But human community inescapably requires institutions and traditions. Without them life would degenerate into chaos and new
forms of bondage. The modern pursuit of liberation from all
social and historical restraints is finally dehumanizing.

Theme 10: *The world must set the agenda for the Church.
Social, political, and economic programs to improve the
quality of life are ultimately normative for the Church's
mission in the world.*

This theme cuts across the political and ideological spectrum. Its form remains the same, no matter whether the content is defined as upholding the values of the American way of
life, promoting socialism, or raising human consciousness. The
Church must denounce oppressors, help liberate the oppressed, and seek to heal human misery. Sometimes the
Church's mission coincides with the world's programs. But the
norms for the Church's activity derive from its own perception
of God's will for the world.

Theme 11: *An emphasis on God's transcendence is at least
a hindrance to, and perhaps incompatible with, Christian
social concern and action.*

This supposition leads some to denigrate God's transcendence. Others, holding to a false transcendence, withdraw into
religious privatism or individualism and neglect the personal
and communal responsibility of Christians for the earthly city.
From a biblical perspective, it is precisely because of confidence in God's reign over all aspects of life that Christians
must participate fully in the struggle against oppressive and
dehumanizing structures and their manifestations in racism,
war, and economic exploitation.

Theme 12: *The struggle for a better humanity will bring about the Kingdom of God.*

The struggle for a better humanity is essential to Christian faith and can be informed and inspired by the biblical promise of the Kingdom of God. But imperfect human beings cannot create a perfect society. The Kingdom of God surpasses any conceivable utopia. God has his own designs which confront ours, surprising us with judgment and redemption.

Theme 13: *The question of hope beyond death is irrelevant or at best marginal to the Christian understanding of human fulfillment.*

This is the final capitulation to modern thought. If death is the last word, then Christianity has nothing to say to the final questions of life. We believe that God raised Jesus from the dead and are ". . . convinced that there is nothing in death or life, in the realm of spirits or superhuman powers, in the world as it is or in the world as it shall be, in the forces of the universe, in heights or depths—nothing in all creation that can separate us from the love of God in Christ Jesus our Lord" (Romans 8:38 f.).

Signers of the Appeal:

Dr. Peter L. Berger
Department of Sociology
Rutgers University

Dr. Elizabeth Ann Bettenhausen, Lutheran Church in America, Department for Church and Society

The Rev. William Sloane Coffin, Jr., Chaplain, Yale University

Father Avery Dulles, S.J.
Department of Theology
The Catholic University of America

Dr. Neal Fisher
United Methodist Church
Board of Global Ministries

Dr. George W. Forell
School of Religion
The University of Iowa

Dr. James N. Gettemy President, The Hartford
Seminary Foundation

*Dr. Stanley Hauerwas
Department of Theology
University of Notre Dame

*Father Thomas Hopko
St. Vladimir's Orthodox Theological Seminary

Dr. George A. Lindbeck
The Divinity School
Yale University

Dr. Ileana Marculescu
Visiting Professor of Philosophy and Religion, Union Theological Seminary

Dr. Ralph McInerny
Department of Philosophy
University of Notre Dame

*The Right Rev. E. Kilmer Myers, Bishop of The Diocese of California, The Protestant Episcopal Church

Dr. Richard J. Mouw
Department of Philosophy
Calvin College

Pastor Richard John Neuhaus
Church of St. John the Evangelist, Brooklyn, N.Y.

*Dr. Randolph W. Nugent, Jr.
United Methodist Church
Board of Global Ministries

Dr. Carl J. Peter
Department of Systematic Theology, The Catholic University
of America

Father Alexander Schmemann
St. Vladimir's Orthodox Theological Seminary

Father Gerard Sloyan
Department of Religion
Temple University

Dr. Lewis B. Smedes
Department of Theology
Fuller Theological Seminary

Father George H. Tavard
Methodist Theological School in Ohio

*Father Bruce Vawter, C.M.
Department of Theology
DePaul University

*The Venerable John D. Weaver, Director of Future Plan-
ning, Diocese of California, The Protestant Episcopal Church

Dr. Robert Wilken
Department of History
University of Notre Dame

*Signers who were involved in the preparation for the Hartford meeting but were not
able to participate in the meeting itself.

For a World
with Windows

Peter L. Berger

Every human event takes place in a historical situation with near-infinite causal antecedents and linkages with other events. This fact provides the livelihood of historians and social scientists. Here the event in question is a statement issued by a small group of Christian intellectuals gathered in Hartford, Connecticut, in January 1975. The considerable attention given to the statement almost instantly may also be regarded as part of the event. Already various critics and commentators have situated the event in different ways: as a resurgence of the Protestant principle, as a counterattack by ecclesiastical reactionaries, as part and parcel of a right-wing wave in America, and so on. Without straining too much, it would be possible to add several additional contexts of the event with at least a measure of persuasiveness. After all, everything human is connected somehow with everything else. Any delineations of context, therefore, must be partial, tentative, and, at least to a degree, subjective. Nevertheless, it is possible to make the following statement with some assurance: The sociocultural context of the Hartford Appeal is one in which there has taken place a widespread loss of transcendence and in which there have been far-reaching accommodations by Christians to this loss. Conversely, the Appeal called for a return to transcendence and for a less accommodating stance by Christians in the contemporary scene. What does this mean?

Imprisoned in Modernity

This is hardly the place to attempt a philosophical or phenomenological analysis of the concept of transcendence. Yet something must be said about it if the following is to be intelligible. It is particularly important to understand that the issue here is not a theoretical one: As I understand it, the concept refers to a type of human experience. Needless to say, quite different concepts have been coined with the same experiential referent: For example, the concept of the supernatural points to the same type of experience (and, by the way, has been far too cavalierly discarded by recent religious thought). Whatever may have been the philosophical and theological weaknesses of his formulations, it was the great achievement of Schleiermacher to have emphasized that religion is, *au fond*, not theory but experience.

Everything that is known historically indicates that this experience is very old indeed, and that it is universal. As far back as there are records, human beings have reported the experience of occurrences, forces, and beings that differ radically from those encountered in ordinary, everyday life—that is, of realities that transcend the reality of ordinary life in a very fundamental way. Now, not all transcendences of ordinary reality (the one that Alfred Schutz called the "paramount reality" or "common-sense reality") can be identified as religious (or rather, if they are so identified, the religious category becomes clumsily broad). Thus the individual transcends ordinary reality in dreams, orgasm, musical ecstasy, and mathematical abstraction. (Much work remains to be done, incidentally, in clarifying wherein these several transcendences differ *and* resemble each other.) The fundamental transcendence at issue here, and generally in the phenomenon of religious experience, has some very distinctive characteristics. They are best summed up by the term "sacredness," and the analysis of this made more than half a century ago by Rudolf Otto continues to be the most useful one. The transcendence of the sacred confronts man with a radical otherness, which nevertheless profoundly concerns him. It puts ordinary life in question, while at the same time it puts this life in a cosmic frame of reference. Perhaps most fundamentally, it indicates that what men know as their world is but the antechamber of an infinitely vaster and "more real" world, in which and through which human life receives its ultimate significance.

In all likelihood human beings have always differed in the degree of openness to this experience. There has probably always been a spectrum ranging from mystics to skeptics, with most men somewhere in the middle, where the sacred realities are intuited or believed rather than directly known. What has changed historically, though, is the place given to transcendence in what may be called the "official world views" of human societies. Through most of history the basic legitimations of both social institutions and individual lives were derived from transcendence: The gods had instituted kingship, divine forces were at work in the acts of sex or of agriculture, the power of the nation was divinely willed, and so on. It is precisely this type of legitimation that has lost credibility in recent history. This loss is the heart of the process called "secularization." Both social institutions and individual lives are increasingly explained as well as justified in terms devoid of transcendent referents. Put differently: The reality of ordinary life is increasingly posited as the *only* reality. Or, if you will: The common-sense world becomes a world without windows.

Virtually everyone agrees that something like secularization has indeed taken place in western civilization during the last few centuries. There are different views as to the causes of this, as to its range and its likely future course. Again, this is not the place to expound and discuss these various views. The following expresses one interpretation, hardly eccentric though by no means agreed to by all the scholarly community (the interpretation is much indebted to Max Weber): The causes of secularization must be sought, primarily, not in movements of ideas (such as the influence of modern scientific thought) but in concrete social experiences. Thus a prime secularizing force is not the abstract rationality of science or philosophy, but the "functional rationality" (a Weberian term) of modern capitalism, bureaucracy, and industrial production. These social formations of modernity bring about habits and mind-sets which are unfavorable to the religious attitude. They encourage activism, problem-solving, this-worldliness, and by the same token they discourage contemplation, surrender, and a concern for what may lie beyond this world. Put simply, modernity produces an awful lot of noise, which makes it difficult to listen for the gods.

To this should be added the causal factor of pluralization. Through most of history people lived in cohesive communities, which provided a stable social-psychological base ("plausibility structure") for meta-empirical certitudes. Modernization shatters or fragments such communities, forcing people to exist in a cacophony of divergent world views and *ipso facto* making moral and religious certainty hard to come by. This means that urbanization and "urbanity" (as carried today by mass education, mass mobility, and the media of mass communication) are also agents of secularization. What is more, looking back to the beginnings of the process some three hundred years ago, secularization has become much more diffused and greatly accelerated as one gets closer to the present time, simply because its various institutional and sociocultural "carriers" have come to be more widely and firmly established.

An interesting question in this connection is whether modern people actually have less experience of transcendence, or whether this experience is only kept more hidden because the "official" world view has delegitimated it. The issue is unresolved. Increasingly, though, the latter interpretation seems to do greater justice to the facts (such as the unanticipated resurgence of religion in thoroughly secularized milieus in Western countries and in the Soviet Union). How one answers this question has obvious bearing on prognostications regarding the process of secularization. If the experience of transcendence is indeed ineradicable in human life, then it will sooner or later reassert itself on the level of legitimations—that is, it will sooner or later "come out of the closet." In that case, secularization is neither progressive nor irreversible.

America has undergone secularization in a distinctive manner. For reasons that cannot be elaborated here, secularization in this country was for a long time milder and less visible than in other parts of the Western world. In other words, for a long time America was, or at least appeared to be, "more religious" (de Tocqueville and others made much of this in their interpretations of America). Again for reasons that cannot be detailed (they all relate to the aforementioned sociocultural "carriers" of secularization), there has been a change in this in the recent past. The society has become more overtly and visibly secular in its "official" self-definitions. This is particularly true of the intellectual scene. No doubt the milieu of the intelligentsia was more secularized than the country at large even in an earlier period. More recently, though, this secularity has expressed itself much more aggressively and, because of the rapid diffusion of intellectuals' views through the channels of the so-called "knowledge industry" (the term was coined by Fritz Machlup), the same secularity has become much more influential. Once more it may be questioned whether this means that there are fewer religious people in the society or whether there is less religious experience. What has happened in the mainline Protestant churches and in Roman Catholicism since Vatican II is quite clear, though: Christian intellectuals and, increasingly, those who shape church policy have taken their cues more and more from the "official reality-definers"—that is, from the highly secularized intellectual elite.

Retranslating Transcendence

This accommodation to secularity may be observed on both the levels of thought and of action. On the first level the accommodation tends to follow this formula: A secular definition of reality is posited as normative and the religious tradition is translated in such a way as to conform to this norm. Since secularity is itself highly pluralized, and since intellectuals more than most people are prone to follow fashions, this formula has been filled with a variety of contents. Thus Christianity has been translated into the terms of existentialism, of psychoanalysis, of Marxism, among other secular world views. In each case, the transcendent elements of the tradition are de-emphasized or put aside completely: Transcendence is translated into immanence. The *real* content of the tradition is then identified with human authenticity, say, or personal fulfilment, or liberation (be it political or psychological). On the level of action, then, the programs of the institutional church are reshaped to maximize these secular goals. Church programs then become experiments in self-discovery, psychotherapy, or political activity, as the case may be. Since the intellectuals are believed to know that such programs will reach modern people "where they really live," the changes are accepted for strategic reasons by church officials who may have some uneasiness or doubts about the theological validity of all this.

This type of accommodationism has, inevitably, led to tensions between the intellectual-bureaucratic elite in the churches and the religiously more conservative lay membership. These tensions have been well-documented in a number of studies (the works of Charles Glock, Jeffrey Hadden, and Dean Kelley, for example). Thus far there has been little outright rebellion. But there has been a broad process of slippage and of revulsion leading to loss of commitment (most visible in recent years in the Roman Catholic community, where the changes were introduced with great suddenness and in the time-honored authoritarian manner). Beginning in the late

1960s there has also been a strong resurgence of strongly transcendent (or, if you will, supernaturalist) religion in America, much of it taking place outside the churches (Jesus People, or the various orientally inspired groups) or taking forms sharply deviant from the accustomed piety of the churches (such as occultism or glossolalia). This resurgence is all the more interesting as its major concentration has been in the most secularized milieus of the society—among the upper-middle-class, college-educated young. It is perhaps too early to differentiate what in all this is a genuine religious revival or a passing fashion. But the fact that most of this new religiosity manifested itself either outside the churches altogether or in forms that must be doubtful in terms of the churches' traditions is noteworthy: It is probable that it is related to the aforementioned accommodation of the churchly elite to a secularized world view. If, needless to add, the current religious resurgences do indeed indicate an outer limit, if not a reversal, of the secularization process, then the churches may have severely undercut their own capacity to shape or participate in the religious wave of the future.

It is in this broad context, then, that the Hartford Appeal must be situated. It was motivated by an increasingly urgent sense of concern about this situation. The response to it indicated clearly that the group issuing the Appeal was not alone in such concern. In this concern, it is safe to say, there was unanimity in the group. And, despite differences in theological outlook within the group, the common response to the sociocultural context provided the crucial element of unity. Thus some in the group perceived the Appeal as a call for a return to the tradition, while others were more concerned with a return to transcendence whatever its relation to tradition. Some saw the focus of the Appeal in its attack on culture religion in all its forms, while others were more concerned with the need to legitimate serious theologizing against the superficialities of current intellectual fashions. All of these interests, however, were welded together by the context just outlined.

Thus the loss of transcendence, as experienced in the socio-cultural context, could be deplored equally by those whose own notion of transcendence was firmly embedded in a traditional understanding of the Christian faith (say, in Evangelical terms) and those more open to the possibility that transcendence might manifest itself in the future in terms that would rupture the tradition.

As it was written, the Hartford Appeal can be directed against the cultural or political accommodation of Christianity in any form, left as well as right. In other words, the Appeal can be used to criticize those who would identify the American way of life with the Christian faith as much as those who would so identify the revolutionary movements of the Third World. This was done very deliberately (among other reasons, no doubt, because few of the drafters of the Appeal were to the right of the liberal center of American politics and several were clearly to the left of it). It was also much emphasized in various explanations and amplifications of the Appeal by members of the group (as, indeed, in this volume). Yet the sociocultural context of the Appeal makes for an important modification of this critical universalism: The right and left versions of culture religion in contemporary America have quite different social locations. Generally speaking, the right version (Christianity as legitimation of the status quo) is very sparsely represented in the "urbane" upper-middle-class world where the "knowledge industry" obtains its personnel and its ideas; its strength is in the lower-middle-class, working-class, and provincial worlds that the intellectual elite despises as "Middle America." Conversely, the left version (Christianity as legitimation of radical social change) is institutionalized in the world of upper-middle-class intellectuals.

This, incidentally, is a very important fact, by no means limited to the area of religion: "Leftism," including Marxism in all its denominations, is largely a bourgeois ideology in the most literal sense—its adherents, at least in the West, are overwhelmingly members of the upper reaches of the bourgeoisie. This characterization may also be applied to Latin America, where intellectuals of this class are usually even better off than their North American cousins: People living in spacious villas, surrounded by high walls with broken glass on top, served by cheap domestic labor—and writing books on revolution. Since this is so—that is, since the most prestigious, avantgarde, culturally elitist versions of culture religion today are of the left variety—it is quite understandable that the Appeal was perceived by many as being exclusively directed against the left. This might well change in the not-too-distant future, if the masses in America should ever succeed in taking political revenge on the "pointy heads" (an eventuality that nobody in the Hartford group would welcome).

In its sociocultural context, then, the Hartford Appeal can best be understood as saying *no* to specific accommodations to secularization, accommodations that can generally be subsumed under the aforementioned formula by which transcendence is translated into immanence. Precisely because this formula is applicable to quite different ideational contents (it is what philosophers call a *Leerformel*), to say *no* may "hit" liberation theology today but tomorrow may be directed with equal force against some new upsurge of pseudoreligious Americanism.

Situating Ideas

Since the argument of this essay is essentially sociological (a somewhat difficult exercise under the circumstances; it is never easy to sociologize about something in which one participates), this may be the place to touch on one question that has been raised about the Appeal: If everything that has been happening on the American religious scene can be sociologically explained, what is the point of trying to go against it? If, that is, "everything is socially determined," why issue an Appeal in the first place? The issue, of course, is just what is meant by "social determination." Every *Zeitgeist* has a sociocultural context which, at least in principle, can be explained. Locating or situating ideas in a context is a basic procedure of the sociology of knowledge, and indeed of historical scholarship. Thus contemporary American secularism has its *Sitz im Leben,* as do resistances to secularism, and the Hartford group also was not made up of individuals existing in a sociocultural vacuum. In this sense all religious and all intellectual events are socially determined, and *ipso facto* sociologically determinable. But this determination is not mechanical, inevitable, or irresistible. Ideas and society always stand in a dialectical relationship to each other: Ideas come out of a context, but they also act back upon that context. Put differently: At different junctures of the dialectical process society determines ideas and at others ideas determine society. The participants in a social event rarely if ever know at which kind of juncture they are standing. (Which proposition may be taken as a sociology-of-knowledge gloss on the biblical mandate to cast one's bread upon the waters.)

Related to this is the notion that intellectuals and their activities are really unimportant. This notion also appeared in criticisms of the Hartford Appeal—here was a group of professors and other academic types, gathered within the ivy-covered walls of a New England campus, letting loose a manifesto—and so what? To a considerable extent this criticism has already been answered by the response to the Appeal. The vastly greater part of it, expressed in some one thousand letters to the Hartford Seminary Foundation and to individual members of the group, came from people with no intellectual or academic credentials. It is quite true: In many cases the manifestos of intellectuals are of interest to nobody but themselves. It seems that the Hartford Appeal is not one of those cases.

But then, of course, there is the further question: Just how is this response to be sociologically situated? Could it be that, contrary to the antifashion rhetoric of the Appeal, it is itself part of a new fashion, that of the new supernaturalism or of a new wave of right-wing reaction? To answer this question fully would require more data on the response than is available now (for example, to date there has been no analysis of the letters received in terms of the social provenance or the views of the writers). But still, some observations may be made now: To be sure, there is something like a new supernaturalism in America today, precisely as a protest against the repression of transcendence undertaken by the cultural elite. There is a highly visible parade of gurus, charismatic leaders, mystagogues of all sorts. But if that is where the fashion is, the Appeal certainly offers no legitimation of it. Rather, it argues that the mainline Christian churches have inadvertently contributed to this "reaction-formation" (the Freudian term suggests itself as soon as one talks about repression) by their accommodations to secularism. If all the churches offer is psychotherapy and politics, no wonder that those who seek God will turn elsewhere. The Appeal is not an endorsement of whatever presents itself as transcendence, but it calls the Christian community to return to the transcendent core of its own faith. It is more arguable whether, in the United States today, there is a right-wing thrust. There is certainly no evidence of that in the milieus of the intellectual elite, where there is a continuation of the overall left tendency of the last decade (it has become a little less strident than it was a few years back—precisely because it has been so successful). Is it possible that right-wingers will take the Appeal as an endorsement of their positions? It is possible, of course. Just about any set of ideas can be bent in different political directions (there are even people who view the oriental despotism of, say, Kim Il Sung as a manifestation of Marxism). But if any would so use the Appeal, they will find it to be a double-edged sword: Its repudiation of culture religion and of the ideological misuses of Christianity will, just about inevitably, cut their own hands.

Finally, the sociological argument of this essay is also relevant to the criticism that the Hartford Appeal attacked "straw men," that the repudiated thirteen themes were caricatures, that no one really said anything like that. This objection can

be empirically invalidated by surveying the theological literature of the last decade. Indeed, if one were to take the trouble
and to risk a little incivility, one could go through the published
works of some of the major critics of the Appeal and find
"proof-texts" for every one of the thirteen themes. But there
is a more basic point to be made: The themes are precisely
"pervasive" in that they reflect a very broad cultural and intellectual climate, shaped by secularization, of which they are
only a small part. This point is lucidly elaborated in Avery
Dulles' essay in this volume and need not be further emphasized here.

Much of contemporary intellectual and indeed political life
makes greater sense if it is viewed in the context of modernization, of the discontents of modernity, and of countermoderniz-
ing reactions. Taking very different ideological and behavioral
forms, there is in much of the world today a struggle between
the myths of modernity and various countermyths. The same
struggle also takes religious and theological forms. The Hartford Appeal, in its broadest context, may be seen as an element
of a critique of modernity that is taking shape. In that sense
it may even be called antimodernist. But, very clearly, it is *not*
antimodernist in the sense of a romantic repudiation of modernity *in toto*. The Hartford group was not made up of romantic
reactionaries, of "nativists," either theologically or politically.
To criticize modernity is not to reject it *in toto*. By the same
token, to call for a return to transcendence is not to turn one's
back on the myriad evils that afflict our immanent existence in
this world. On the contrary, as in previous periods of history,
a transcendent point of reference provides a broader perspective on history and one's own situation in it. Thus it provides
a basis for action that is clear-sighted. Those who are captive
to the *Zeitgeist* are finally as limited in their political acts as
in the range of their thought. Whatever one may say about
their theology, they suffer from a myopia of historical and
social vision which inevitably restricts their capacity to act
effectively within their own situation.

A Battle for
Theology

GEORGE A. LINDBECK

The attempt to place the Hartford Appeal for Theological
Affirmation in the broad sweep of Christian history is both
inevitable and problematic. It is inevitable because, whether
we like or dislike the Appeal, we cannot help thinking of
parallels from the past. That is simply part of the process of
understanding and evaluating it. It is problematic, however,
because there are many ways to do this, and all of them seem
arbitrary.

What we shall do in this essay, therefore, is start with some
of the most banal and questionable comparisons. Secondly, we
shall look at the unique features of the Appeal, those aspects
which make it resist easy classification. This leads to a third
section in which a particular and perhaps novel way of looking
at certain types of historical developments, of which the Hartford Appeal seems to be a part, shall be proposed. We shall
conclude with an assessment of the Appeal in terms of this
perspective.

Organizing History

Historical taxonomies tend to be dyadic or triadic, Manichaean or Hegelian. Contemporary American reflexes in these matters are perhaps most often Manichaean: minorities are right, and majorities wrong; establishments cannot be good, nor rebels evil. We are inclined to think in these patterns because our perceptions have been molded by the civil rights movement, by the struggle for liberation in Latin America, and by the protests against the war in Vietnam. In all these cases, so the opinion-makers in the mainline churches generally believe, protesting minorities have been right against torpid Christian majorities in alliance with oppressive establishments.

These generalizations may hold well enough in their original *Sitz im Leben,* but they create difficulties when applied to the whole of history. Then they prompt automatic suspicions of the Christian mainstream, whether Catholic, Protestant, or Orthodox, and tempt us uncritically to applaud sectarians and dissenters of all kinds. Another response is to painstakingly reinterpret the founders of major traditions as failed revolutionaries who became pillars of new and deleterious establishments once their causes were successful. Jesus was actually a Zealot, Paul a fighter against the early Jewish-Christian majority, Aquinas a heretic from the point of view of the Augustinian establishment, and the Reformers would really have been on the Anabaptist side if they had had the courage of their basic convictions.

These currently popular ways of looking at history can be used, obviously enough, to attack the Hartford Appeal; but we need to notice that they can also be used to defend it. The signers are inclined to view it as a protest against a liberal intellectual establishment that has capitulated to the dominant cultural forces of the present and that now represses the impulses toward transcendence which still struggle in the bosoms of ordinary folk both inside and outside the churches.[1] From this perspective, the Appeal stands with Jesus against the Sad-

ducees, the cultural accommodators of their day, whose surrender to Hellenism had left the common people without responsible shepherds and prey to the Pharisees on the one hand, and
to power-hungry revolutionaries on the other.

Like every analogy, however, this one fails to walk on all
fours. The common folk about whom Jesus was concerned
were economically and politically oppressed, while the common folk in our contemporary middle-class American churches
certainly are not. Furthermore, the Sadducees dominated the
ecclesiastical institutions of their period, while our present
intellectual accommodators are especially strong in the
academy.

Thus it takes no great inventiveness to twist this bit of
dichotomous thinking into an attack on the Appeal, and to
classify it as just another reactionary move from a comfortable
majority against an adventurous minority. It is, to be sure, more
sophisticated than most such moves. It does not condemn
outright the prophetic protesters, but its effect, nevertheless,
is to undermine the struggle against oppression by focusing on
a peripheral issue. It is almost as if the pre-Civil War evangelical abolitionists had allowed themselves to be distracted from
the fight against slavery by dislike of New England transcen-
dentalism, or as if the Reformers had turned from their attack
on Rome in order to oppose humanism.

These ambiguities suggest that there is something fundamentally wrong with dividing the world into conservatives and
liberals or reactionaries and progressives. Perhaps a triadic
categorial scheme works better. Not only Hegel, but also the
Reformers thought so. They typically read the struggle for the
truth of the Gospel in tripartite, not dualistic terms. Unfaithful
Christians divide into a right and left (for example, into papists
and enthusiasts), but true faith opposes both. Both capitulate
to culture, to the wisdom of this world, but in different ways.
The radical right blindly defends a dying culture, an outmoded
system; while the radical left, in its rage against moribund
traditions, is open to every new wind of doctrine, every fad and

fashion, especially if it promises utopia or paradise. Both use the Christian message simply as a source of proof-texts for their culturally derived certainties. They distort and contort it to support their reactionary or antinomian passions. Neither respects its integrity or searches for its autonomous word. In short, neither theologizes. They do not seriously try to hear and interpret what the Gospel says independently of our desires and preconceptions about God, ourselves, and the world in which we live. They trust, so the Reformers put it, not in Jesus Christ, the *verbum externum*, but in the inner word which they call the Spirit—or, sometimes, "Jesus within"—(although for the reactionaries, the Spirit is institutionalized, while for the enthusiasts, it is supposed to be spontaneous). Thus, as Luther vividly said of the papists and anabaptists of his day, they are like foxes pulling in opposite directions but tied together by their tails. On this view, then, the cause of Christian faithfulness in every generation is to resist cultural captivity whether on the right or the left, and to harken to the biblical story, climaxing in cross and resurrection, which stands in tension with all our human thoughts and wishes.

This tripartite taxonomy is more complex than a dichotomous one, and so it is not surprising that it makes more sense of the complexities of history. This is particularly true when it is used dynamically, as by Hegel, in order to take account of the cumulative, noncyclical character of history. The cause of truth is not a *via media* between extremes, between thesis and antithesis, but is rather something fundamentally new, a synthesis in which the old reactions and progressivisms are both abrogated and *aufgehoben*. For those who are so inclined, it is satisfying to think in this pattern not only of the Reformers, but also of Jesus (over against Sadducees and Zealots), of Paul (against Judaizers and spiritualists), and of Aquinas (against Archbishop Tempier on the right and Averroists on the left). Finally, and triumphantly, the Hartford Appeal seems to fit beautifully. It battles both reaction and accommodation in the name of that which transcends both.

The only difficulty is that, as in the case of dyads, one can sort out the triads of history—especially when they are contemporary—in a variety of ways. The Corinthian spiritualizers could have made out a plausible case for themselves as representatives of creatively faithful Christianity over against both Paul and the Judaizers; and something analogous holds for the Anabaptists in the sixteenth century, as well as for some of the types of accommodation which the Hartford Appeal opposes. Furthermore, aren't there occasions when simply standing fast (reaction) is a defensible position? That's what the confessional conservatives, who stood to the right of Barth, did in the Confessing Church's struggle against Nazism; and one could argue that it is this kind of position to which the Hartford Appeal is most nearly allied. In short, it seems that the data of history can be organized in many different ways, and that the choice between them is whimsical.

We have not by any means exhausted all the conventional classificatory schemes. We have said nothing, for example, about reform in the sense of "return to the sources"; nor about classical Catholic theories of development modeled after Aristotelian syllogistic deduction; nor about those theories, such as the one Cardinal Newman proposed, which liken certain kinds of change to organic growth and to the emergence of oak trees from acorns. It might be possible to understand the Hartford Appeal either *pro* or *con* in terms of any one of these patterns, but our main point in this section has probably already been made at sufficient length. As the medievals said of *auctoritas*, the nose of history is made of wax and can be pushed in any direction.

We shall return to this problem in the third part of this essay, but first we must look at the Appeal in and of itself, and try to identify, not how it resembles other events in the history of the church, but rather what is unique about it.

Never Before

The Hartford Appeal is *sui generis* because it battles for the possibility of theology rather than itself proposing a theology. It does not affirm, but rather asks for affirmation; it does not theologize, but rather calls for theology; it does not confess the faith, but rather pleads that it be confessed; it does not present any particular version of the Christian Gospel, but simply points to some features which any version should have. There is, for instance, no particular Christology or doctrine of God in it, although it implies that doctrines of God and of Christ are necessary. Similarly, it does not define what it means by resurrection or life in the world to come, but simply insists that their affirmation in some form or other is imperative.[2]

This, it would seem, differentiates it from all previous theological group manifestoes. These assumed, it would appear, that everyone, including the opposition, agreed on the possibility of Christian theology. They agreed that there is a distinctive Christian message in at least some measure independent of time and space. The debates, therefore, were on the articulation of that message and on its correct or erroneous interpretation. The quarrels between right and left, majorities and minorities, orthodox and heretics were over the right theology, not over the possibility of theology *tout court.* Opponents were often accused, to be sure, of destroying the possibility of authentically Christian faith or thinking, but it was the falsity of their affirmations that did this, not the absence of affirmation. This was the complaint of St. Paul against the Judaizers and spiritualizers, of Athanasius against the Arians, of Luther against the papists and Anabaptists, of Barmen against the *deutsche Christen.* The complaint of each side against the other was that of doing theology wrongly, not of failing to do theology at all.[3]

It is because the Appeal concentrates simply on the latter point that it is wrong, contrary to *Time* magazine,[4] to think of the themes it repudiates as heresies. They are not propositions that anyone affirms in the unqualified form in which they are rejected. Virtually no one seriously and explicitly maintains without reservation that "Modern thought . . . is superior to all past forms of understanding reality" (Theme 1), or that "The world must set the agenda for the Church" (Theme 10). But these are widespread *Tendenzen* which inhibit the theological attempt to discern what is true and right from an independently Christian perspective. Many of the signers at Hartford admit that they personally find these themes seductive. They also inhibit the signers from making theological affirmations, whether true or false. They so completely discourage theology that they even prevent explicit heresy. The Appeal, so it could be said with only some exaggeration, cries out for theology of any kind, even heretical theology; and such a plea is unheard of in any previous epoch of church history.

The explanation for this novelty is in a way obvious although, as we shall see, its significance is not easy to assess. We are more aware than preceding generations of the cultural determinants of theology. We have become convinced through historical research, and such disciplines as the sociology of knowledge, that every theology and theologian is captive to culture. The fact of captivity is, of course, not new. The people of God under both covenants have been from the beginning in Babylonian exile. In prior epochs, however, reformers and protesters have thought that they could return to the Promised Land; or, at the very least, that they could free themselves while in exile from alien influences and learn again to sing the songs of Zion in accents undefiled. We (or at least the supposedly learned among us) no longer think this. We know that we shall live out our lives in Babylon using foreign tongues in business and at home, in synagogue and church, transforming them, no doubt, but also being transformed. The meanings of the patriarchs and prophets, of Jesus and the apostles, can never be recovered unalloyed. Further, we are likely to add, this is just as well, because those meanings, contextually conditioned as they also were, are inapplicable to our situation. In short, we are inescapably doomed—or perhaps commissioned—to cultural captivity.

There are three ways of responding to this captivity. We may delude ourselves into thinking that we are free of it, willingly capitulate to it, or struggle against it. Delusion, needless to say, is not escape. Those on the right who insist that theirs is simply the old-time Gospel confuse their grandparents' words (for example, Dwight L. Moody's) with the *ipsissima verba* of the Lord. Popular or folkloric conservatism, some recent studies indicate, is typically of this character: what was new seventy or a hundred years ago tends to be identified by the masses, in modern as in ancient times, with immemorial truth. This may be harmless enough on occasion, but when it is consciously maintained in the face of massive evidence to the contrary, it is a matter of bad faith. This is why theological conservatisms of the present day often lack the integrity of the past positions which they revere and profess to preserve.

While the Hartford Appeal clearly warns against this blind cultural captivity on the right, its main attention is focused on the opposing leftist temptation to embrace with open eyes whoever or whatever happens to be the latest victor in the cultural wars. This, however, is the end not only of the actuality, but of the possibility of theology. Theology, as we have already suggested, has no reality unless it is somehow or other independent, normed by its own norms, specifically by the story of Jesus, rather than by criteria external to Christianity itself. The capitulators, in contrast, make of their culturally derived convictions a Procrustean bed into which they fit the faith.

It should be noted that, from the viewpoint of this analysis, the Appeal's emphasis on transcendence is historically conditioned and in a sense accidental. The neglect or denial of transcendence happens to be a currently pervasive trait of our society; but one can easily imagine that the climate of opinion in another time or place might lead to an equally un-Christian and untheological obsession with transcendence and negation of immanence. In that case, an analogue to the Hartford Appeal might appropriately reverse the present emphasis. It was, after all, the humanity of God, not his otherness, which was the central issue in the days of Nicaea.

The Hartford statement appeals for a third position, one which, in a tripartite scheme, would be described not as midway between right and left, but as opposed to both. The power of culture is to be neither denied nor embraced. We should not delusively imagine on the one hand that the language of Zion is unaffected by the alien tongues which we inevitably employ, nor, on the other, suppose that these tongues, however useful or enriching they may be, are somehow superior to that of prophets and patriarchs, of Jesus and the apostles. The struggle for theology, for the independence of the message, must go on, but in a new and culturally self-conscious way.

We should remember that the problems which evoke this plea, while they may have become in our day uniquely acute, are by no means entirely new. They have been growing for at least two hundred years. Rapid change has combined with awareness of historical and cultural relativities to undermine traditional authorities; and this has led to denigration of the old, exaltation of the new, and fascination with futurity. In the past liberal period, however, theology still had a place. Christian optimists may have been sure of the inevitability of progress, but their notions of progress were professedly defined by extramodern norms—at the very least, for example, by the ethics of Jesus. Their positions, therefore, were still within the arena of theological argument, and were open to counterarguments such as those in Schweitzer's *Quest* or Barth's *Römerbrief*.

That, however, has changed. The present mood is apocalyptic rather than gradualistically progressive, and confidence in reasoned argument has faded. The progress which the liberals treasured—defined as it was in scientific, technological, industrial, and *laissez faire* democratic terms—is now rightly attacked. Only sweeping discontinuities and radical ruptures with past ways of thinking, feeling, and behaving, so it is said, can save us. So-called conservatives share this attitude no less than radicals. And it is common to Pentecostalists and flag-waving premillenialists, to ecclesiastical technocrats with their eager attention to the latest therapeutic or organizational recommendations of the behavioral and administrative sciences, and to counterculturalists and oriental religionists. None do theology: some because they lack all notion of what constitutes intellectually responsible thinking; others because personal or social needs have replaced abiding Christian truth as the ultimate theological criteria. In short, so the Hartford signers apparently believe, the possibility of theology is threatened now as never before, and it is on this that they concentrate their attention.

Yet—and this is another peculiarity—they do not try to prove that theology is in fact possible. They propose no theory, no method, for how to go about doing it. They do not try to refute rightists who claim that there can be no Word of God if there are errors in the Bible, or leftists who have succumbed to the scandal of particularity (who cannot believe in the finality for human time in space of an obscure Jewish rabbi in Roman Palestine). This very lack of theological argument, however, made it possible for strange bedfellows to join together in appealing for theology. Traditional Thomists who believe in building on natural theology, Tillichians who favor correlation, Rahnerians, French theological structuralists, law-and-gospel Lutherans, and Barthians who oppose all these positions (not to mention Wittgensteinians, Whiteheadians, Pannenbergians and Palamists) could all sign the Appeal (and in many cases did). Insofar as there is an argument in the Appeal, it consists simply of a listing of the contemporary themes which inhibit theology. It is almost as if the authors supposed that their mere articulation would unmask their prejudicial character and thus unleash the *anima Christiana naturaliter theologica* for its endeavors.

It seems from this catalogue of peculiarities that the uniqueness of the Hartford Appeal is rather greater than that which is common to historical events in general. It is the kind of uniqueness which breaks normal categories and creates bewilderment. It strives—whether successfully or not—to redraw the map of controversy. To the degree that theological affirmation, the very possibility of theology, has become a crucial issue, the familiar dichotomies between right and left, conservative and liberal, pietist and Social Gospeller are losing their usefulness. They no longer indicate where the fundamental struggles lie. Only if one remembers this is it possible to understand the strange agglomeration of conservative evangelicals, Roman Catholics, Eastern Orthodox, and mainline Protestants which assembled at Hartford.

This very uniqueness of the Appeal, however, suggests where we should look for parallels: not to other pleas for affirmation (there are none), but to epochs when patterns were broken, when everything was in flux and transition. There have been, so both the conventionally and unconventionally wise of our day agree, only a few periods in the last two thousand years of Christian history when changes comparable in magnitude to the present ones have been in process. The transition from Judaism to Hellenism and, as time went on, from persecuted minority to imperial majority might be cited. Then there were the growing rift between East and West, the twelfth- and thirteenth-century developments, the Reformation cataclysm, the rise of liberalism in the nineteenth century, and now, close on the heels of that, the collapse of liberalism together with older surviving patterns.

In each case, it will be observed, the fundamental debates were different. The relation to Judaism was central in the first transition; Christological dogma in the second; soteriology, especially in its individual anthropological dimension, in the Reformation; and revelational epistemology in the period of liberalism. Now, if the Hartford Appeal is correct, the problem is that of the possibility of theology, of distinctively Christian affirmations of any kind.

The similiarities between theological actions in various periods is formal rather than material, functional rather than substantive. Our task in the next two sections will be to see the sense in which this is true, and what light, if any, this sheds on the Hartford Appeal.

Shifting Paradigms

What we need to do, if our comments about the Appeal's uniqueness are correct, is to concentrate on the structural similarities of periods of major transition and of revolutionary change. This, by the way, is not what historians of the church and of doctrine have customarily done. They have emphasized the dissimiliarities between transitional periods by, for example, contrasting the Hellenization and "Constantinianization" of Christianity in the first centuries with the reverse processes which have been going on now at least since the Reformation. This tends to turn the earlier development into a warning, a negative example, an instance of decline and fall from the true faith. Perhaps, however, by focusing on resemblances we will be able to garner some positive lessons on how a religion such as Christianity retains its identity even when established patterns of thought and life disintegrate and quite new *Gestalten* take their place.

The model which I shall outline (with outrageous brevity) for understanding transitions within a religion is adapted from T. S. Kuhn's now famous book, *The Structure of Scientific Revolutions.*[5] He borrowed it in part from work in sociology and aesthetics,[6] but in applying it to the development of science, he articulated and clarified it in such a way that it has gained new usefulness in the analysis of revolutionary changes of all kinds.[7]

Let us try to think, then, of major transitions as defined by what Kuhn calls "paradigm shifts." Such shifts occur when concrete instances of theological activity, forms of piety, or ecclesiastical structure, which had long served as paradigmatic instances of how a religion—in our case Christianity—should be interpreted in thought and life, lose their guiding and organizing power and are replaced by others (providing, that is, the religion does not disappear or lapse into ossified archaism). Thus, to cite some examples, Platonic theology, Augustinian introspective piety,[8] and the papacy—as it had developed by the time of Gregory the Great—have served as paradigms for much of Christendom from late antiquity through the middle ages and down into modern times. They have inspired a wide diversity of cognitive, experiential, and ecclesial patterns in different situations. Similarly, Lutheran, Calvinist, Eastern Orthodox, and free church paradigms can be distinguished whose implications have been developed in a staggering variety of ways.

It can be seen from these illustrations that not every major change within a religious tradition involves a paradigm shift. Indeed, paradigms can be models for change and thus may retain their power through vast transmutations. Augustine—not to mention Paul or Jesus or Buddha—has molded the thinking and behavior of multitudes in very different times and cultures and with exceedingly diverse concrete consequences. Yet one set of consequences need not necessarily be considered more authentically Augustinian than another. It may be that the difference is more in the situation than in the paradigm. Similarly, in physics, Newton's work remained overwhelmingly paradigmatic during close to three centuries of astounding developments. In both science and religion, progressive and cumulative change is dependent on continuities in "a research tradition transmitted by key historical examples of exemplars."[9]

In order to understand this point, we must bear in mind that a paradigm, as is indicated by the grammatical origin of the word, is not a pattern whose details are to be reproduced, but is rather a normative illustration of proper method, of how to handle new as well as old cases and data. Thus a new world may come into being while the paradigms through which worlds are construed remain basically the same. The paradigms function somewhat like spectacles: the landscape alters and we see radically different things, but the interpretive medium remains unchanged. Or, perhaps more aptly, the paradigms are like an exemplary use of language or an exemplary body of literature. One can learn from them the appropriate vocabulary, grammar, and rhetoric for dealing effectively with a multitude of topics which they never mention. (To be sure, there may also be experiences and realities beyond the scope of the paradigms, but more of that later.)

These analogies may help us to understand the power of paradigms. Like language or aids to vision, they enlarge rather than restrict our ability to cope with the world. They are the instruments which enable human beings to interpret and organize the raw data of social, personal, and intellectual life. They provide the principles of order by which we build a cosmos out of chaos, and thus overcome the sheer confusion and meaninglessness which is the greatest of all threats to human life and dignity. From infancy to old age, human beings have an appetite for models which is no less compelling, even if less palpable, than the hunger of the starving for food. Paradigms, whether in religion or science, are far too valuable to be jettisoned lightly.

Yet paradigms do have their limits, and paradigms fail. Social, cultural, and intellectual changes may occur which can no longer be effectively construed by means of the inherited exemplars. They may then be experienced as oppressive rather than empowering. The institutional, experiential, and cognitive grammars and vocabularies of the past may prove incapable of saying what needs to be said. They may lack the resources to identify, much less solve, the new problems that arise. As Kuhn says in reference to science, anomalies accumulate which the old theories cannot handle. Thus Paul, Athanasius, Augustine, Aquinas, Luther, and Calvin were forced to forge new theological languages in which to discuss the unprecedented issues with which they were confronted. They built on the work of exemplary predecessors (for example, Augustine on Paul, Cyprian, and Ambrose) and then, in turn, became exemplary for later generations.

As can be seen from these examples, the relation in religion as well as science between theory and praxis (or between superstructures and infrastructures) is more Weberian than Marxist. Infrastructural changes on the cultural, psychosocial, behavioral, and organizational levels may undermine the usefulness of old paradigmatic ways of conceptualizing and symbolizing the faith, but they do not by themselves produce a revolution, that is, a new, paradigmatic theological vision. The infrastructural changes are of little enduring importance to a religion (except, perhaps, to weaken or destroy it) unless they are embodied and legitimated in a new and persuasive vision. Thus the connection between theory and praxis in a religion such as Christianity is powerful but indirect. Institutional structures, for example, may persist through theological revolutions, as Roman Catholicism illustrates, but their functional character will then, at least in the long run, be profoundly modified; and conversely, as Protestant sectarianism abundantly shows, radical institutional discontinuities, given the appropriate paradigms, are compatible with considerable theological stability.

It will also be observed that, in Christianity as in science, continuities persist through revolutions. Western science has retained certain perspectival or "grammatical" features (such as the stress on intersubjective testability or "objectivity") as well as elements of "vocabulary" (for example, the "themes" of which G. Holton speaks)[10] ever since its birth among the Greeks. In the case of Christianity, the most obvious persistent factor has been the biblical saga of a people and the world summed up and climaxing in Jesus. These two types of continuity are, to be sure, very different. Jesus might be called the foundational paradigm in Christianity, and there is obviously no comparable figure in science. Yet in both cases, the elimination of certain publicly identifiable abiding features would mean the end of science and Christianity respectively.

Revolutions in Christianity, we are now in a position to specify, occur when the Christian story is organized and utilized in markedly different ways in order to structure and interpret new life worlds and new thought worlds. The cross, for example, became central in the Western milieu of the introspective conscience, formed by the interaction of Roman law and biblical Torah under the influence of a paradigmatic tradition of Pauline interpretation stretching from Augustine to Luther. In the East, to cite a well-worn contrast, the resurrection retained its primacy (even while losing much of its Messianic thrust) in a world oriented toward metaphysical speculation and cosmic contemplation.

Enough has now been said to indicate that a theological revolution, like a scientific one, is not to be equated simply with the abolition of a previously regnant order. That is not genuine revolution, but dissolution, the descent into chaos. For this reason, contrary to popular stereotypes, scientists, like theologians, are highly resistant to changing their dogmas, their fundamental theories and outlooks, even when these are unsatisfactory, unless they can be persuaded that better ones are available.[11] The new theories or paradigms may be very different from the old, but they do what the old did and even more.

This point enables us to distinguish between good and bad, or authentic and inauthentic revolutions. The bad variety occur when the new paradigms account for a lesser range of data than the old ones. Sometimes it is not the internal logic of development, but external pressures, whether cultural, psychosocial, or political, which impose new paradigms. Lysenko's eminence in Soviet biology is a recent scientific example, and much of the Neo-Thomist revival, spurred as it was by papal fiat, is perhaps a theological one.[12] For the most part, however, inauthentic revolutions in religion are hard to identify except in extended historical retrospect. We may be reasonably sure that Gnosticism in early Christianity was an alien cultural imposition in view of the extreme cognitive violence which it did to the biblical story and its inability, in contrast to early Catholicism, to legitimate cohesive and large-scale communities; but what should we say about the sudden rise of Neo-Orthodoxy and its equally sudden decline? Has Barthianism, for example, lost popularity because of its intrinsic inadequacy as a Christian proclamation to the contemporary situation, or has this happened because cultural accomodation has made mainline churches and theologians resistant to full-orbed presentations of the Gospel? Such questions are resolved as much on the level of praxis as of theory, and therefore take time to settle.

Nevertheless, an analysis of the structure of theological revolutions does provide some guidelines. As we have already said, an authentic revolution absorbs rather than abolishes the past, not in some vague quasi-Hegelian synthesis, but in the sense that it does what was previously done, and more. The new paradigms may, to be sure, be radically novel in form. In science, for example, the earth now moves around the sun rather than *vice versa*, and space and time are relative rather than absolute. Much, however, remains unchanged: Archemides' discoveries still hold in mechanics; Galileo's formulae for velocity and acceleration continue to function near the surface of the earth; and Newton's laws of motion remain quite satisfactory for macroscopic, slow-moving processes. This suggests that an authentic theological revolution, *mutatis mutandis*, is one which comprehensively affirms the heritage even while reformulating, redirecting and extending it into new domains of experience and reality. It is, as Augustine, Aquinas, and the Reformers all illustrate, a return to the sources and not only an adjustment and assimilation of the new.

A further related characteristic of a good paradigm shift is that it is not premature. It grows, so to speak, out of the soil of once fruitful, but now exhausted positions. Sharp conflict with the past is, to be sure, likely. Distorted or dessicated versions of old positions will be defended beyond their period of usefulness, and uncertainty regarding the proper pattern of the new breeds polemics rather than civil argument. This happens even in science during major theoretical transitions. But break-throughs come only from exploring the full potentialities of the earlier phase. It was, for example, only by extending the Newtonian research program to its utmost limits, as in the Michaelsen-Morley experiments testing the "absurd" theory of ether, that the precise anomalies were uncovered which made Einstein's work both necessary and possible. What Kuhn calls "normal science" must complete its task before a fruitful revolution can occur. Similarly, so it would seem, the "normal" theological work of struggling seriously with both the strengths and weaknesses of the tradition is a necessary precondition for constructive paradigm shifts.

In terms of these criteria, there are not many examples of fully successful revolutions in the history of Christianity. Even St. Paul's success may be questioned. One can argue, to be sure, that in principle he provided a new and exemplary Gentile way of being a Christian which was reconcilable rather than opposed to Jewish Christianity, and he retained, rather than abolished, the eschatological, covenantal, and "this-worldly" thrusts of the Jewish heritage; but his success, if success it was, was quickly aborted on the practical level by the cultural barriers between Greek and Jew. Gentile Christians did not long retain the full Pauline vision. Protestants customarily point to the decline of the *sola fide,* but a more fundamental defect is that Hellenistic incarnationalism tended to abrogate rather than incorporate Hebrew messianism. Similarly, the Reformation paradigms, despite their manifest superiority to much of what they replaced, failed at point after point to deal adequately with ranges of experience and doctrine which their Catholic predecessors had been well aware of. Luther's ecclesiology, for example, did not have functional equivalents to the Roman safeguards against Erastianism; and Calvin, despite his occasional efforts to the contrary, seriously shortchanged the sacramental, ritual, and aesthetic dimensions of human life. One can, if one wishes, blame St. Paul's failures, and to some extent those of the Reformers, on extraneous cultural and political factors rather than on inadequacies of theological vision; but that does not alter the fact that revolutions in the sphere of religion seem regularly to involve losses as well as gains. Lesser transitions, such as those represented by Augustine or Aquinas, were in some ways more satisfactory in moving into the future while preserving the relevant past, but then the crises they surmounted were less acute.

This is an absurdly sketchy account of the structure of theological revolutions, but it does perhaps suffice for drawing some useful practical conclusions. It helps us resist the inclination to suppose that there is anything intrinsically good or bad in minorities or majorities, establishments or antiestablishments, conservatism or progressivism. It all depends, as traditional Marxism also had the good sense to see, on whether the time is ripe for revolution. Radical extremisms of the right or left are, to be sure, never good. It is never helpful to lapse into blind reaction on the one hand, or, on the other, into the antinomian rage to destroy existing order without taking responsibility for what might replace it. Even here, however, contexts make a difference. During periods of unbroken and developing order, the antinomian left may need to be listened to as the voice of the oppressed; but during major crises, it can become simply destructive of the possibility of humane existence for everyone. Conversely, in the first of these situations, reaction is likely to be irremediably bad, the petulant anger of dispossessed elites; while in the second, although always dangerous, it may at least have the excuse of trying to fend off the chaos which destroys human meaning and decency for the little ones as well as the great ones of this world.

Finally, it will be observed that there is no utopianism in this view. Progress is not inevitable. There is no guarantee that when one set of paradigms becomes inadequate, a new and better set will be found. A religion (whatever might be true of science), may prove intrinsically incapable of adjusting to new circumstances, and ossify or disappear; or the training, skill, patience, and creativity to discover revitalizing forms may be lacking. It is with this sobering thought in mind that we now turn, once again, to the Hartford Appeal and the contemporary religious situation.

Forever Normative

Some of the questions that remain belong to the scientific study of religion, while others belong to theology. From the first of these perspectives, we need to ask how the Hartford Appeal is to be evaluated if it is looked at as an incident within a period of transition; while from the second, it should be judged by distinctively Christian norms. Believers and unbelievers might agree completely in principle on the first count, while on the second, the unbeliever would either disagree or declare himself incompetent to express an opinion.

It should be clear by now that the Hartford Appeal makes eminently good sense if viewed as an event within a paradigm shift (and that, needless to say, is one of the reasons which prompted this essayist's attempt to use Kuhn's work). When old paradigms seem increasingly inadequate and new ones implausible, it is tempting to deny the necessity or possibility of theology. This, however, is like giving up science simply because one is in the midst of a transition. The Appeal is addressed precisely to this danger. It does not try to propose either a new or old theology. In the present circumstances, that would be divisive. It rather tries to rally together those who believe that theological affirmation is vital to Christianity. It asks Christians to attend seriously to past theological affirmations, and to recognize that these are better than nothing during our period of waiting and struggle for something new. It appeals to those who, while open to the new, believe that this will develop out of critical and careful work with the old, rather than its uncritical abandonment. On the other hand, it opposes those who, having turned from theology, take their guidance from movements which are not responsibly rooted in the Christian tradition. It is thus precisely the kind of ecumenical action which is appropriate if we are in fact in the middle of a shift where the old paradigms are faltering under an accumulating weight of anomalies, and new and more effective ones have not yet clearly emerged.

There is, to be sure, nothing inevitable about this conclusion; but the debate over its correctness is wholly nontheological. It depends on a certain reading of the empirical situation and on the adequacy of a paradigm-shift analysis of theological crises. There is no reason why religious convictions should determine the outcome. Hindu, Marxist, humanist, and orthodox Christian scholars might very well be on both sides of the issue. No matter what one's theological views, one might agree or disagree on social-scientific grounds with the proposition that the Appeal correctly articulates what a religion such as Christianity needs at the present time for its continuing identity and credibility.

There are also, however, specifically theological issues raised by the Hartford Appeal. These arise when one asks about its legitimacy, not from the viewpoint of the scientific study of religion or of some ideological analysis of the contemporary situation, but in terms of the internal logic of the Christian faith. *Immobilisti* might try to argue from Scripture or tradition, for example, that the Appeal underrates the immutability of theological formulations. We shall assume for the purposes of this essay, however, that their case depends on irresponsible proof-texting, on eisegesis rather than exegesis. The more serious theological challenge comes from the left. Is not orthopraxis rather than orthodoxy, action rather than theological affirmation, absolutely fundamental? What about, for example, Matthew 25: 31–46? Is not the struggle against oppression and for liberation basic, and is it not the sin against the Holy Spirit to discourage, distract, or divide those engaged in it by talk of the dangers of alien influences, the importance of "transcendence," and the need to keep

Christian language straight and its grammar uncorrupted?

This critique cannot be ignored. Biblical studies combined with the waning of previous paradigms (hellenistic, Constantinian, medieval, and Reformation) have opened our eyes to the primacy of praxis and of the struggle for human liberation. Furthermore, the social sciences have helped unmask for us the emptiness of much orthodoxy and of much theological affirmation. Over and over again the Christian story of suffering and triumphant love has been used to rationalize and legitimate the most dire cruelties and oppressions. This history of the failures of Christian faithfulness, even in the best periods of theological affirmation, is something Hartford does not stress, and it can for that reason be read triumphalistically. It can far too easily be understood as a plea to return to the good old days when right proclamation blossomed unimpeded in works of revolutionary love; but there never were any good old days, not even in New Testament times.

The Appeal, like any brief manifesto, has many insufficiencies, but this is theologically the most serious. It should have emphasized more strongly that theology is by no means the most important thing in Christianity. It stands low in the hierarchy of values. Perhaps I Corinthians 13 should have been paraphrased to the effect that theology without love is like "a sounding gong or clanging cymbal." And, furthermore, does not the love of which we speak require that we stand with the oppressed against the oppressors even when the oppressors are ourselves?

This emphasis, however, in no way diminishes the need for theological affirmation, but simply puts it in its proper place. That place is not in the apex, but in the foundations. Theological reflection on right affirmation is useful in somewhat the same way that thought about adequate diet is sometimes necessary to love, or lexical and grammatical considerations are necessary to masterpieces of truth, beauty, and goodness. The Scriptures themselves assume the need for theological learning. The prophets do not oppose erudition in the Torah, but rather its misuse. Early Christians represented Jesus as learned above all rabbis at the age of twelve, and Paul was a master of the tortuous complexities of Talmudic reasoning.

When one asks why theology has this essential, though subordinate place, the case for the Appeal is equally clear. Theology is necessary to praxis, concepts to percepts, doctrine to the discrimination between true and false liberation. In reference to the last point, it may be suggested that no one would decry the need for hard and detailed reasoning from Scripture, tradition, and science apart from the belief that he or she already knows from other and superior sources what putative oppressions are real and which of the professedly liberating forces are to be supported. To rely on these other sources, however, when they are interpreted theologically, is to be a spiritualist, *Schwärmer,* or *illuminati.* It is, in the conceptuality of St. Paul and the language of Luther, to set the interior inspiration of the Spirit above the *verbum externum,* that is, the narrative of God's dealing with the world summed up in Jesus Christ.

In conclusion, then, the theological case for the Hartford Appeal is that the affirmations for which it calls are forever necessary because Jesus Christ as witnessed to in Scripture and tradition is forever normative for human thought and life. The nontheological student of religion can say part of this. It is tautological to affirm that as long as Christianity retains a recognizable identity, the Jesus of Scripture and tradition will be central for it. Faith goes beyond this, however, and clings to the hope that there will always be a remnant, through this and all ensuing revolutions in theological paradigms, which proclaims in deed no less than word that the God of our Lord Jesus Christ is Lord, Judge, and Savior of all humankind.

Notes

1. On the repression of the transcendent, see Peter Berger, "The Devil and the Pornography of Modern Consciousness," *Worldview* (March, 1975), pp. 36–37.

2. A number of the comments on the Hartford Appeal underlined its "non-credal" character: see, e.g., the editorial in *Commonweal* (Feb. 14, 1975), p. 379.

3. One can, to be sure, find apparent exceptions to these generalizations. Luther, for example, attacking Erasmus in *Bondage of the Will* says, *Tolle assertiones et Christianum tullisti* (WA 18, p. 603). It could also be argued that from the point of view of Barmen, the *deutsche Christen* did not simply have a bad theology, but no theology—i.e., no distinctively Christian position. Nevertheless, both Luther and Barmen went much beyond the Hartford Appeal not in simply calling for theological affirmations, but actually making them.

4. Feb. 10, 1975, p. 47.

5. Kuhn, T.S., *The Structure of Scientific Revolutions*, 2nd ed., Chicago: University of Chicago Press (1970).

6. As he himself says, *op. cit.*, p. 208. See also his "Comment [on the Relations of Science and Art]," *Comparative Studies in Philosophy and History*, XI (1969), pp. 403–412.

7. A remarkable example of such an application in the field of social and political revolutions is the unpublished Ph.D. dissertation of John Peter Gunnemann, "The Moral Meaning of Revolution," Yale, 1975.

8. See Krister Stendahl, "St. Paul and the Introspective Conscience of the West," *Harvard Theological Review*, 56 (1963), pp. 199–215.

9. The phrase is borrowed from Ian G. Barbour, *Myths, Models and Paradigms: A Comparative Study in Science and Religion*, New York: Harper & Row (1974), p. 133. Barbour concentrates on what I later call "founding paradigmatic figures" (e.g., Jesus) rather than, as does this essay, on successive paradigmatic interpretations of a single continuous religious tradition.

10. *Thematic Origins of Scientific Thought*, Cambridge, Mass: Harvard University Press (1973).

11. On the dogmatism of science, see Kuhn, *op. cit.*, pp. 132, 136, and John Ziman, *Public Knowledge: The Social Dimension of Science*, Cambridge, England: Cambridge University Press (1968), p. 22: "I wonder whether the failure of Science to grow in China and India was due as much to the general doctrinal permissiveness of their religious systems as to any other cause. Toleration of deviation, and the lack of a very sharp tradition of logical debate may have made the very idea of a consensus . . . in the Philosophy of Nature . . . absurd. . . ."

12. I do not mean to equate the two cases except, perhaps, in the instance of the very rigid and narrow Neo-Thomism of the "Twenty-four Theses" approved in 1916 by Benedict XV.

Unmasking Secret Infidelities

Avery Dulles

The notion of ecumenism is flexible and ill-defined. In the literature most familiar to me, ecumenism is described in terms of relationships among Christian churches; though some authors prefer to speak in this connection of communions, confessions, or denominations rather than churches. All seem to agree that ecumenism implies positive and nonpolemical relationships. Some would see the ecumenical movement as directed primarily to the visible union of Christians in one Church with a single profession of faith and a single organizational structure. Others understand ecumenism in more general terms, as an effort to foster cordial or fruitful relationships among the churches by methods such as joint confessions of faith, common worship, or cooperative action. It seems to me that all these forms of association may properly be designated as ecumenical, even though not intended to lead toward visible union among the churches themselves.

A few authors would wish to extend the term ecumenical to relationships between Christians and Jews, or more generally to relationships among all faiths or religions. While I can see nothing objectionable in this wider usage, I shall, in deference to the more common practice, adhere to the narrower usage explained in the preceding paragraph.

The Hartford Appeal makes no mention of ecumenism, yet it has been hailed as an ecumenical break-through. In a lead editorial entitled "Ecumenical Theology at the Crossroads," *America* commented that if the challenge of the Hartford Appeal is picked up, "ecumenical theology will be well on its way to establishing its own agenda for the next decade."[1]

While I would not go so far as to contend that the Hartford Appeal is the charter of a new ecumenism, I do believe that the statement represents a significant and in some respects original ecumenical contribution. The purpose of this chapter will be to explore the ecumenical implications of the Appeal.

Ecumenical Authorship

In some very rudimentary sense of the word, the Appeal may be described as ecumenical insofar as it proceeds from a group of Christians belonging to different church bodies. The Hartford meeting of January 1974 was organized by two Lutherans, Peter L. Berger and Richard John Neuhaus. It was hosted by the Hartford Seminary Foundation, in the person of its president, James N. Gettemy of the United Church of Christ. The eighteen participants at the conference included six Lutherans, five Roman Catholics, two Orthodox, two Christian Reformed, and one representative each from the Methodists, the United Church of Christ, and the Presbyterians.

No special significance can be attached to this break-down by denominations, since the theologians were invited as individuals, not as representing their respective communities. Further, the list of invited participants, and even of those who were expected to attend, differs slightly from that of the actual participants. Thus it was not planned or expected that there would be a total absence of Episcopalians and Baptists, as turned out to be the case. As a matter of fact, two of the

Episcopalians who had been invited but were unable to attend, subsequently asked that their names be added to the list of signers.

A few critics of the Hartford Appeal claim to have found in it a strong impress of certain denominational positions, such as the Lutheran "two kingdoms" doctrine or the Barthian concept of transcendence.[2] As a signer, I am convinced that the language was deliberately chosen so as to be free from all such limited perspectives. In their discussions the Hartford theologians did not generally group according to their denominational affiliation. By common agreement certain proposed formulations were ruled out as being too exclusively tied to a particular confessional tradition.

The Hartford theologians spoke as individuals and made no effort to represent any constituency. For this reason their personal theological orientation is probably more significant than their denominational affiliation. By and large, the group may be described as moderate or centrist. Although a few of the signers might fairly be called conservative, and several others are generally classified as liberals, there were no extremists either from the right or from the left. Thus the Hartford Statement is indicative of the positions of certain theologians from the mainline churches who are situated somewhere near the center of the theological spectrum. Given its totally private and unofficial character, the Appeal could not by any stretch of the imagination be described as a consensus statement of the churches or denominations represented at Hartford.

Can a statement by a privately selected group of individuals from different confessional groups be properly designated as ecumenical? Some seem to assume that the bureaucratically structured form of ecumenism is alone worthy of the name. The Hartford signers would wish to contest exactly this assumption. The carefully balanced representation of different confessional bodies in the conciliar ecumenical movement frequently makes for very bland statements that fail to embody any challenging insights or points of view. The Hartford Appeal, which seeks to be balanced in the sense of avoiding simplistic exaggerations, has at least the merit of being pointed in a definite direction. For this reason it has found a greater echo among the general public than have most statements emanating from the headquarters of the World or National Council of Churches. The Hartford signers do not claim to be an institution, but they dare to look upon their work as a prophetic beginning.

The Ecumenism of Theological Dialogue

Quite apart from the make-up of the group who authored it, the Hartford Appeal should be characterized according to its content. Does it address ecumenical questions, and if so, does it fit into any of the known categories of ecumenism?

The two most common forms of ecumenism in the past generation have been: the ecumenism of theological dialogue in the tradition of faith and order, and that of common action in the tradition of life and work. The Hartford Appeal must therefore be examined in relation to each of these traditions.

The ecumenism of theological dialogue flourished in the great World Conferences on Faith and Order, especially those of Lausanne (1927) and Edinburgh (1937). Since Montreal (1963), the Faith and Order Commission of the World Council of Churches has focused its attention more on contemporary and secular issues, but the traditional theological dialogue continues to go on in bilateral and multilateral consultations, generally undertaken by joint action of the denominations concerned. The bilateral consultations that have occurred since Vatican Council II have resulted in a number of important consensus statements, the findings of which have begun to feed back into faith and order studies, to the great advantage of the latter.[3]

The primary objective of this theological ecumenism has been to overcome the doctrinal differences that have separated, and continue to separate, the communions. The Hartford Appeal is not itself an instance of this kind of dialogue. Since the focus at Hartford was not on the doctrines that divide Christian confessions from one another, the Appeal had no occasion to comment on the problem of Christian unity. Several of the Hartford themes, however, have clear implications for the conduct of ecumenical theological dialogue.

Theme 5 repudiates the proposition, "All religions are equally valid; the choice among them is not a matter of conviction about truth but only of personal preference or lifestyle." As it stands, this statement refers to relationships, not between Christian confessions but between Christianity and other faiths. But the principle would seem to be applicable, in a proportional way, to those profound doctrinal divergences that have brought about the major rifts within the Christian family. Of them also it may be said that the issues are not mere matters of personal taste. To hold that they were no more than this would be to "flatten diversities and ignore contradictions." Thus, in the language of Theme 5, we may apply to inter-confessional relations the statement: "Truth matters; therefore differences among religions are deeply significant."

From the words already quoted, it might appear that Theme 5 calls for a renunciation of the effort at mutual understanding and appreciation that has characterized the ecumenical movement; that it favors a return to the sterile polemics of the past. This interpretation, however, would be incompatible with the added explanation, which states: "We affirm our common humanity. We affirm the importance of exploring and confronting all manifestations of the religious quest and of learning from the riches of other religions."

Applying this principle proportionally to intra-Christian ecumenism we may say, in the spirit of Hartford: "We affirm our common Christianity. We affirm the importance of exploring and confronting all manifestations of Christian existence and of learning from the riches of traditions other than our own." In setting forth this principle, I am admittedly going beyond the letter of Hartford, but I am expressing what seems to me to be both valid in itself and consonant with the Appeal. Ecumenism, in my judgment, can scarcely be practiced without the recognition that the various branches of Christianity, as well as the various religions, have much to offer and to receive from one another.

Mutual criticism and mutual enrichment would be prevented if the differences among the confessions were trivialized to the point of eliminating all tensions. To assert that the Catholic and the Protestant, the Anglican and the Orthodox really agree, or that their differences are unimportant, is profoundly unecumenical. It is an insult to all the communions. In effect, it makes nonsense of religion itself and implies that no religion really has anything intelligible to say.

In pointing out the unecumenical character of such exaggerated irenicism, the Hartford Appeal aligns itself with Vatican II's Decree on Ecumenism, in which we read: "Nothing is so foreign to the spirit of ecumenism as a false conciliatory approach [*falsus irenismus*] which harms the purity of Catholic doctrine and obscures its assured genuine meaning."[4]

The assumption here is of course that Christian doctrine can have a genuine and established meaning. At this point, Theme 5 interlocks with Theme 2, which rejects the idea that "religious statements are totally independent of reasonable discourse." As the explanation goes on to say, "A religion of pure subjectivity and nonrationality results in treating faith statements as being, at best, statements about the believer." If this view were correct, ecumenism would be at an impasse.

The Hartford Appeal makes no attempt to set forth a full methodology of ecumenism. And yet it gives several valuable hints as to the ways in which the existing confessional bodies can go about assessing what is acceptable in the traditions of other bodies and thus supplementing, and even correcting, what is deficient in their own particular tradition.

Theme 2 states very generally that the criteria, while by no means independent of reasonable discourse, are not the same as those of scientific rationality. The view that there is no real knowledge except of measurable objects is one of the illusions of modern empiricism that needs to be dispelled. Reason can reflect upon the data of spiritual experience as expressed in the stories and symbols of the Bible, the liturgy, and the traditional confessions of faith. The developments of any religious tradition are not to be absolutized, but are to be carefully scrutinized for their authenticity and adequacy, with a view to transcending the limitations of past and present formulations.

Theme 1 suggests one method of criticism: to reflect on the degree to which the cherished traditions of a particular denomination are tied to the thought structures of a particular time or culture. This theme affirms the need for Christian thought "to confront and be confronted by other world views," since all are necessarily provisional.

A further technique for overcoming the conflicts between denominational traditions is suggested by Theme 4, which concerns itself with historical reason. It asserts that "Jesus, together with the Scriptures and the whole of Christian tradition, cannot be arbitrarily interpreted without reference to the history of which they are a part." In other words, historical method can arrive at some firm conclusions regarding the original thrust of Christian faith, and these must be made normative for what is alleged to have evolved from them. Instead of arbitrarily refashioning the biblical message in accordance with our contemporary preferences, we must strive to correct our preferences in accordance with the revelation actually given in Christ.

From these few indications I have selected from the Hartford Appeal, it should be evident, I think, that while the Appeal does not attempt to design a program for theological ecumenism, it gives valuable hints as to how such ecumenism might best be pursued. By implication, it takes seriously the existing doctrinal divisions among the separated Christian communions; it favors mutual concern and receptivity among the churches, and condemns certain extreme positions that would render the ecumenical dialogue unnecessary or futile.

The Ecumenism of Social Action

The second major current of ecumenism is interchurch collaboration in the service of human values, especially in the social order. Many theologians in the tradition of Nathan Söderblom have thought that through practical collaboration in the pursuit of justice and peace Christians of different traditions could best be brought into those relationships of trust and understanding that would make it possible for them subsequently to discuss and solve their doctrinal differences. In the past decade, there has been a growing tendency in World Council circles to maintain that "secular ecumenism" is to be pursued for its own sake, even if it does not lead to visible church unity. At Uppsala in 1968 the dominant theme was the Church's power and responsibility to contribute to "the renewal and unity of mankind."[5] "In a world where the whole of mankind is struggling to realize its common humanity, facing common despairs and sharing common hopes, the Christian church must identify itself with the whole community in expressing its ministry of witness and service, and in a responsible stewardship of our total resources."[6] Inspired by Uppsala, the Faith and Order meeting at Louvain in 1971 took as its theme "Unity of the Church—Unity of Mankind." The Faith and Order meeting at Accra in 1974, following up on this theme, accented the Church's responsibility to assist in promoting the eventual unity of the whole human family. "An ecclesiastical unity which would stand in the way of struggles of liberation would be a repressing unity, hindering the just interdependence which Christians are called to serve."[7]

The Hartford Appeal is sometimes thought to have rejected secular ecumenism and to have called for a religion of noninvolvement in the anguish of the world. A distinguished theologian, in a letter to the *New York Times* (unpublished, as far as I know), declared: "I fear that the well-intentioned Hartford Appeal does not set forth 'orthodox concepts of God' (as the [*Times*] article says) at all, but a mixture of gnostic dualism and private piety. Ironically, in its condemnation of religious fads, it pushes the churches toward what your article correctly sees as the 'major adjustment' to the new 'national mood' of retreat from concerns about bigotry, greed, and war."

These charges are totally unwarranted. The Hartford Appeal at many points stresses the importance of social concern and social action. Several quotations should make this clear.

Theme 7 calls for "serious and sustained attacks on particular social or individual evils."

Theme 9 recognizes that institutions and traditions are often oppressive and that they must for this reason "be subjected to relentless criticism."

Theme 10 affirms that "the Church must denounce oppressors, help liberate the oppressed, and seek to heal human misery."

Theme 11 states: "Christians must participate fully in the struggle against oppressive and dehumanizing structures and their manifestations in racism, war, and economic exploitation."

Theme 12 declares: "The struggle for a better humanity is essential to Christian faith and can be informed and inspired by the biblical promise of the Kingdom of God."

In view of these reiterated expressions of social concern it seems irresponsible to accuse Hartford of promoting "gnostic dualism and private piety" and of encouraging a "retreat from concerns about bigotry, greed, and war." The emphasis on a lively sense of the transcendent, which dominates the Hartford Appeal, is in no way contrary to social concern. Theme 11 points out that it would be a false idea of transcendence that would induce one to "withdraw into religious privatism or individualism and neglect the personal and communal responsibility of Christians for the earthly city." According to the traditional understanding accepted at Hartford, transcendence implies the presence of God to "all aspects of life" (Theme 11). To banish God from his own creation, exiling him to some ethereal realm, would be in effect to deny his transcendence.

Once this has been clearly recognized, it is correct to add that the Hartford Appeal cannot easily be fitted into the patterns of "secular ecumenism" according to certain models recently proposed in the World Council of Churches. The difference is indicated in the enunciation of Theme 10, beginning with the words: "The world must set the agenda for the Church." In denouncing this theme, the Hartford Appeal deliberately sets itself in opposition to a trend that was popular in some World Council agencies in the late sixties. For example, a 1967 report of the Department on Studies in Evangelism, drawn up in preparation for the Uppsala Assembly, contained the statement: "The message and structures of the churches can only be formulated with respect to the immense variety of actual realities in amidst which we live. *Hence it is the world that must be allowed to provide the agenda for the churches.*"[8]

This report makes reference to a prior article by Walter Hollenweger, Executive Secretary of the WCC Department on Studies in Evangelism, the concluding paragraph of which reads as follows:

Find out the agenda of the world! Ask the people outside the Church: What are the issues of today? Where does it hurt? Do you expect something from us, and what? In the communities of the churches we always talk amongst producers without ever taking into account our customers. We produce—not unlike those manufacturers in Russia—goods which nobody asks for: stuffed animals, bears, giraffes, elephants. Sometimes we change sizes and colors, but basically it remains the same. They get stored in the *thesaurus ecclesiae.* How could we know what the people need? How can we find out the agendas of the world if we deliberately throw the experts of the world out of our committees?[9]

The idea that the Church ought to receive its agenda from the world, although not explicitly repeated by the Uppsala Assembly, was allowed to color Section II of the *Uppsala Report*, entitled "Renewal in Mission," as may be seen from the quotations already given. This section emphasized that the Church exists for the sake of "others" and that missionary priorities must be continually revised because the world is always changing. As one of the criteria for determining priorities, it suggested that mission should encourage Christians to "enter the concerns of others to accept their issues."[10]

When the slogan "the world provides the agenda" was originally coined, it served to bring out a neglected truth; namely that the Church, while adhering to the Gospel, has to keep its eye fixed on the mutations in secular culture in order to address appropriately the people of a given age and condition. This the Hartford theologians would gladly affirm. It must also be acknowledged that the Church, as a human organization, has much to learn from the world in which it carries on its mission. God speaks to us not simply through the Bible, ecclesiastical documents, and pastoral leaders, but also through the "signs of the times," as Jesus pointed out to his adversaries.

Speaking for myself as a signer of the Hartford Appeal, I would agree with John C. Bennett that there is a "grain of truth" in the discarded slogan. As he says, "It is often interaction with the world that has enabled the churches to gain new understanding of the meaning of their own faith."[11] His illustration of the principle of religious liberty is a case in point.

On the other hand, as Professor Bennett himself says, the slogan is rightly rejected. Etymologically, and according to the first dictionary definition, "agenda" means "things to be done." The slogan therefore seems to mean that the world should tell the Church what the Church is to do. This would be a serious violation of right order. In fidelity to its mission, and in service to Christ its sole Lord, the Church cannot allow itself to become a tool of groups that do not share the Church's goals. If it simply carries out the bidding of non-Christian coalitions, the Church ceases to perform that distinctive service for which it is uniquely qualified.

The Church does not exist to help any particular groups, whether "haves" or "have-nots," to achieve their own special interests. It exists for the sake of the kingdom of God, and in service to the kingdom it must invite all persons and collectivities to repentance and conversion. Not satisfied with a reshuffling of power and wealth, to be accomplished by social revolution, the Church looks forward to a total transformation of man and creation, to be accomplished by the power of God. A reshuffling of earthly resources may at times be called for, but it will not achieve justice in the long run unless human hearts are renewed by God's grace in Jesus Christ. Recognizing this, Hartford in no way disapproves of the Church's involvement in the quest for justice, but insists that such involvement must be informed by the full resources of the Christian tradition. In this way, as Pannenberg has perceived, the Hartford Appeal points the way toward a livelier liberation theology than has yet emerged.[12]

The Church, then, does not exist to respond to the demands placed upon it by any social or economic class. Even the popular notion that the Church ought to respond to the questions put to it by the world is profoundly misleading. Jesus refused to answer many of the questions addressed to him, especially those prompted by curiosity, hypocrisy, or a vain desire for self-justification. Instead he put questions to his questioners. The Church, likewise, must question the world's questions, and in this way challenge the values and priorities on which those questions are based.

Drawing its inspiration, then, from the Gospel, and fully conscious of its specific mandate, but at the same time closely in touch with the actual human situation, the Church must chart its own course. Far from responding to all the requests made of it, the Church must be prepared to say "no," to move against the grain, to set its own agenda. This it can do if the leaders of the Church are both deeply committed to Christ's lordship and deeply engaged in the life of the communities to which they belong.

In criticizing a particular current in the recent literature of certain World Council agencies, the Hartford signatories had no wish to discredit the World Council as such. Still less were they spurning the ecumenical movement. To oppose an ill-advised trend in ecumenism is, in fact, to make a positive ecumenical contribution.

The Ecumenism of Common Witness

In addition to the two main forms of ecumenism discussed in the preceding pages, there is a third, which has received less attention. We may call it the ecumenism of common witness. As a basic description we may take the following quotation from Vatican II's Decree on Ecumenism: "Before the whole world, let all Christians profess their faith in God, one and three, in the incarnate Son of God, our Redeemer and Lord. United in their efforts, and with mutual respect, let them bear witness to our common hope, which does not play us false."[13]

The Hartford Appeal does not fall purely and simply into ecumenism of this third category; it is not a common declaration of faith. Although the Appeal presupposes a body of shared convictions among its signers, it makes no effort to summarize what they believe in common. No mention is made of the basic dogmas of the Trinity and the Incarnation. The authors, all of whom presumably accepted the great creeds of Nicaea and Constantinople, felt no need to draw up a new statement of faith—though they did not deny the desirability of composing new creeds and confessions especially suited to the times in which we live.

The faith has frequently been professed in negative form by means of condemnations. Since the Council of Nicaea, official anathemas have been drawn up against opinions judged incompatible with faith. In more recent times, the popes have repeatedly issued condemnations such as Pius IX's Syllabus of Errors (1864), the anti-Modernist documents issued under Pius X (1907–1910), and Pius XII's repudiation of the *"nouvelle théologie"* (*Humani generis*, 1950). On the Protestant side, the aberrations of the "German Christians" were eloquently condemned by the Barmen Declaration of 1934.

It might have been possible for the Hartford Conference to draw up a list of recent theological opinions that were seen as dangerous or heretical—for example, certain new interpretations of the divinity of Christ or of the meaning of his resurrection. Some reporters, in fact, wrote up the Hartford Appeal as though it had been a summons to orthodoxy. In view of the present polarization between liberals and conservatives in nearly all the churches, it is easy to understand how the impression arose that Hartford was a conservative manifesto directed against certain unnamed liberal theologians. Hartford, however, was not directly concerned with orthodoxy and heresy, in the sense of true and false doctrine. It does not descend into the arena of detailed theological debate; still less does it condemn particular theologians. Even when it touches on such themes as the resurrection and the mission of the Church, the intention is not to endorse some specific theological option but rather to safeguard the very possibility of truly theological discourse.

The journalistic caption, "The Hartford Heresies," could therefore be misleading; and yet, in a sense, the Appeal is very much concerned with heresy. In a well-known essay on the subject, Karl Rahner points out that heresy in our time is taking on a new pattern.[14] In former ages, he says, the mental world of the individual was determined for the most part by things he could explicitly know. Hence heresy assumed the form of propositions contrary to God's revelation in Christ. Today, we live in an age when the mental universe of the individual is largely determined by a tissue of assumptions that make up the public mind of the day. We are immersed in, dependent on, and influenced by a mental world that lies largely beyond our control. Many of the unspoken assumptions of our culture are out of harmony with Christian faith. Thus we imbibe from our environment a kind of latent or implicit heresy. If we were to give objective conceptual expression to everything present in our minds—including our prejudices, attitudes, preferences, and inclinations—we would find ourselves uttering propositions at variance with the faith of the Church.

Rahner points out that because this latent heresy has a tendency to remain implicit it is all the more dangerous. Such heresy is very difficult to distinguish from legitimate trends and from authentic contemporaneity in one's understanding of faith. At times, Rahner observes, latent heresy is to be found simply in "the false proportions, the wrong dose"—in an undue emphasis that can scarcely be verified by objective measurements.[15]

In addition to Rahner, several other writers have anticipated the Hartford Appeal in attempting to identify those prevalent assumptions of our culture that, in their impact on Christians, give rise to latent heresy. In one of the preliminary meetings before the Amsterdam Assembly of the World Council of Churches, the Swiss theologian, Emil Brunner, submitted a list of eleven axioms of contemporary proverbial wisdom that stand in contradiction to biblical and Christian conviction. Inspired by this list, groups in several countries prepared lists of axioms, which are printed in one of the volumes of the Amsterdam series.[16] This direction of thought, however, seems not to have been further pursued within the World Council. Private theologians have occasionally followed this line. James Hitchcock's controversial book, *The Decline and Fall of Radical Catholicism*, has an appendix entitled "26 Heretical Attitudes." Some of the positions he formulates are similar to the thirteen themes of the Hartford Appeal.[17] These resemblances are the more significant because, to the best of my knowledge, no one at Hartford was consciously following either the Amsterdam volumes or Hitchcock's work.

Common Threat, Common Response

The effort to grapple with latent heresy is probably the most striking dimension of the ecumenism of the Hartford Appeal. The official ecumenical movement, as represented by the World Council of Churches and by many regional and local councils, has largely forsaken the task of confronting the new paganism.[18] Theological ecumenism, as represented by the bilateral consultations, has concentrated on special doctrinal questions that have arisen out of the divisions of the eleventh and sixteenth centuries. Neither of these two main currents of ecumenism shows any sign of addressing itself to the massive problem posed for all the churches by the rampant immanentism, humanism, secularism, psychologism, sociologism of our age—a convergent movement that leaves no room for the transcendent except as a kind of psychological "peak experience." Among recent ecumenical efforts, the Hartford Appeal stands alone in confronting the dominant cultural patterns. Whereas other ecumenical efforts tend to be as accommodating as possible in their pursuit of a general consensus, the Hartford Appeal stands out as a self-consciously controversial document. In setting out to unmask the secret infidelity at work in both our popular and our academic culture, the Hartford Appeal almost invites contradicton.

The literary form of the Hartford Appeal has given rise to two persistent objections, which seem to require some notice in the present context. The first objection is that almost nobody, or at least almost no Christian, holds the repudiated propositions. There is some validity to this objection. It is of the very nature of latent heresy to resist explicit formulation. As soon as one articulates the principles or premises that seem to be implied, almost everyone begins to say, "That is not what I hold." The very act of moving to explicit assertion thus evokes disclaimers.

An example may serve to clarify this point. Few Christians, I suppose, would say that the question of life beyond death is marginal or irrelevant—the last of the thirteen themes—and yet many seem to act as though they believed that the only salvation worth considering must be attainable in this world before death, if not by ourselves, at least by some future generation. The very exercise of asking ourselves whether we subscribe to this view can prove medicinal. Once we have explicitly reaffirmed the Christian understanding of salvation, we see the ambiguity of our previous behavior. We are alerted to the apparent implications of our silences and omissions, our enthusiasms and boredoms, our approvals and disapprovals. We often find evidence of tacit heresy in our own lives and in the lives of Christians whose professed beliefs are unexceptionably orthodox.

This brings us to the second objection: that the Hartford Appeal is an act of ecclesiastical triumphalism. It is accused of setting the Church somehow above the world and above history. This impression can only rest on a hasty and inaccurate reading. The whole point of the Appeal is to call attention to errors that are truly pervasive, in the sense that they infect practically everyone, whether Christian or non-Christian, Protestant or Catholic, Anglican or Orthodox. The introductory paragraph expressly declares that debilitating themes are at work within the Church, undermining its ability to perform the tasks to which it is called. The Hartford Appeal, therefore, is not an act of self-congratulation but a summons to the Church to turn to the authentic source of its own life.

We may conclude, then, by attempting to characterize the ecumenism of the Hartford Appeal. It may be described as a common attempt by Christians of various traditions to identify certain widely pervasive assumptions that, if accepted, can scarcely fail to undermine the vigor and integrity of Christian faith and witness. To point out these threats is, I believe, an authentic form of ecumenism, and one that differs from nearly everything that has been identified with ecumenism in the past. Because the threat is a common one, the churches will be well advised to work together in seeking to meet it. Only by a joint response to the assumptions that tend to obscure the reality of the transcendent can the churches hope to respond adequately to the present crisis of faith. The new style of ecumenism provided by Hartford is urgently needed, not as a substitute for more familiar types of ecumenism, but as a necessary supplement. With the Hartford Appeal ecumenism is invited to seize the initiative and, as the *America* editorial puts it, to establish its own agenda.

Notes

1. *America* 132/6 (Feb. 15, 1975), p. 103.

2. See, for instance, the responses respectively of Harvey Cox and of Gregory Baum in *Worldview* 18/5 (May 1975), pp. 26–27 (Baum on neo-Orthodoxy) and 23 (Cox on the two kingdoms).

3. Examples are afforded in the booklet, *One Baptism, One Eucharist and a Mutually Recognized Ministry* (FO Paper 73) (Geneva: WCC, 1975). The last two of these three studies are heavily indebted to the bilateral consultations.

4. *Unitatis redintegratio* 11, in W. M. Abbott (ed.), *The Documents of Vatican II* (New York: America Press, 1966), p. 354.

5. N. Goodall (ed.), *The Uppsala Report* (Geneva: WCC, 1968), p. 14.

6. *Ibid.*, p. 36.

7. *Uniting in Hope* (FO Paper 72 on the 1974 Commission meeting in Accra), "Statement of the Conference," p. 93.

8. W. J. Hollenweger (ed.), *The Church for Others* (Geneva: WCC, 1968), p. 20 (italics supplied).

9. W. J. Hollenweger, "Agenda: The World," in "The World Provides the Agenda" (Papers from the Birmingham Consultation), *Concept* XI (Geneva: WCC, 1966), p. 20.

10. *Uppsala Report*, p. 32.

11. J. C. Bennett, "Silence on Issues of High Priority," *Worldview* 18/5 (May 1975) 24.

12. W. Pannenberg, "Breaking Ground for Renewed Faith," *Worldview* 18/6 (June 1975) 38.

13. *Unitatis redintegratio* 12, in W. M. Abbott, *Documents*, p. 354.

14. K. Rahner, "On Heresy" in his *Inquiries* (New York: Herder and Herder, 1964), pp. 403–463, esp. pp. 437–463.

15. *Ibid.*, p. 460.

16. Emil Brunner's list of axioms, followed by lists of axioms from Great Britain, America, Germany, and France, may be found in the volume, *The Church's Witness to God's Design* (volume 2 of the Amsterdam series,

Man's Disorder and God's Design, London: SCM Press, 1948), pp. 80–84. The "Axioms from America" afford interesting points of convergence with the Hartford Appeal.

17. J. Hitchcock, *The Decline and Fall of Radical Catholicism* (Garden City, N.Y.: Doubleday Image Books, 1972), pp. 187–189.

18. About the same time that the Hartford Appeal was issued, the veteran ecumenist, W. A. Visser 't Hooft published a brief article, "Evangelism in the Neo-Pagan Situation," *International Review of Mission* 63 (1974) 81–86. Visser 't Hooft describes very accurately the immanentistic nature worship that permeates the religiosity of our time.

Reason, Relevance
and a Radical Gospel

GEORGE WOLFGANG FORELL

Shortly after the Hartford Appeal for Theological Affirmation received wide publicity, a former student and friend of mine who serves as pastor of a congregation in a small town in Iowa was returning with the local funeral director from a funeral he had conducted. It should be remembered that a mortician in a small town has the opportunity to listen regularly and frequently to sermons by clergy of all religious persuasions. No one who is at all interested in the subject has a better chance to evaluate the theological atmosphere in a community.

In the course of the conversation my friend learned that the undertaker had been much impressed by the Hartford Appeal. He exclaimed that he was grateful that some theologians were finally making sense and expressing beliefs to which he could assent. His curiosity aroused, my friend pursued the subject further only to discover that the mortician was enthusiastic about all the themes which the signers of the Hartford Appeal had described as false and debilitating. At least this one reader —superficial, to be sure—of the Hartford Appeal agreed wholeheartedly with every one of these themes.

Traveling about the country discussing the Appeal with individuals and groups across the West and Midwest, I became aware that the themes do in fact describe a good deal of the "religious consensus" among many people superficially attached to the religious establishment, at least in its Protestant manifestation. Indeed, the angry reaction the Appeal elicited, especially among some of the clergy associated with colleges and universities, indicated that a sensitive spot had been touched. Later, talking to friends in Europe, especially in West Germany where the Appeal had been widely disseminated, I learned that there, too, it was seen as a document which addressed a pervasive religious mood.

The question arises: What went wrong with Protestant thought—which has its roots in the Bible, stresses Pauline theology, depends on the seminal insights of an Augustine, and finds its classical articulation in the writings of Luther and Calvin—that made it so susceptible to the religious cant summarized in these thirteen themes?

The following pages are an attempt to offer one answer to this question. It is hoped that it will further the discussion and encourage others to suggest both modifications and new and better answers. It is written from a particular point of view, represented in the Hartford group but by no means the only or even the dominant one.

Preoccupied with Unreason

The claim that "religious statements are totally independent of reasonable discourse" pervades the religious atmosphere. One might try to derive it from Luther's tendency to depreciate reason and refer to it occasionally as "the devil's whore." But as any reader of the sources will remember, Luther's concern was to liberate theology from its fatal enslavement to philosophy,[1] and his critical statements about reason deal with it when used as a means to reach certainty about God. Such statements could easily be balanced by other utterances extolling reason as an essential tool in all human efforts, including religious communication. It was the utter irrationality of the enthusiasts of his time, the people he called *Schwärmer*, who depended for their authority on direct inspiration, which drove Luther to sarcastic remarks about men like Thomas Münzer, of whom he said that he sounded "as if he had swallowed the Holy Spirit, feathers and all."

Luther himself tried to reason with his opponents. His style was forceful and often sarcastic. He tended toward hyperbole, but he was trying to persuade. Even his frequent use of paradoxical formulations was for him a persuasive device, from the assertion of a theology of the cross in his Heidelberg disputations to the insistence, in his later writings, on the human being as righteous and sinner at the same time.

As far as Calvin is concerned, his effort to use reasonable persuasion so dominates his *Institutes of the Christian Religion* as to be exemplary. Thus, while the religious polemic of the period was often vicious and ready to use the cheap *ad hominem* argument, it remained an effort at reasonable discourse. The opponents were clearly aware of the other person's intent; they disagreed violently, but they tended to understand each other nevertheless. In fact, they not infrequently borrowed each other's best arguments and modified them for their own use in the ongoing controversy. Deplorable as the tenor of the religious debate was, it revealed a common universe of discourse.

It would take us too far afield to trace the development of the preoccupation with unreason in Protestant thought and to attempt to identify the period when the respect for reason was lost to Protestantism. But it would seem that the increasing preemption of reason by the rising modern science, especially in the nineteenth century, forced the Protestant defenders of religion, in whose environment its new world view was advancing, into a defensive position which rejected reason in favor of feeling. This resulted in a bifurcation of the theological enterprise. There have always been and there are now academic theologians of Protestant background who use reason with great skill and devotion in order to articulate their idiosyncratic theological perspective. Their efforts, however, proceed independently of the Protestant movement. Their books are only read by a small elite and have no discernible effect on the life of the Protestant churches.

Indeed, the striking feature of the contemporary religious situation which the Hartford Appeal addresses is the apparent absence of reasonable discourse. Not only are most religious arguments totally incomprehensible to the outsider, who simply ignores them (they have no "apologetic" significance), they are almost equally nonsensical to the committed member of the Christian movement who attends church regularly. This is as true of the statements of the mod-theologians as of the so-called fundamentalists. It has produced the reaction among churchgoers of "turning off" the sermon, since it is no longer a form of understandable communication. Indeed, thousands of regular attendants at Protestant church services are in the habit of ignoring what goes on in the pulpit for twenty or thirty minutes and engaging instead in their own religious or secular meditations, since it is simply impossible to follow many sermons as a form of rational discourse. Among some Protestants it is the frequent recurrence of some "approved" words which establishes the acceptability of the sermon. These words may be moralistic or biblical cliches among the so-called fundamentalists, or sociological, psychological, or political cliches among the mod-theologians. But it is the occurrence of the "approved" words rather than their reasonable connection which validates the address.

Perhaps the so-called "Gospel of Christian Atheism" may serve as an example of what is commonly called the religious "left." There the "good news" is that the human story is "a tale told by an idiot, full of sound and fury, signifying nothing." "Christian" means the denial of Jesus as the Messiah and the assertion that he was the paradigm of the ultimate loser, and "atheism" means "pantheism."

But the absence of reasonable discourse is not less striking, though perhaps less surprising, on the religious "right." Here faith becomes credulity and the "faithful" compete with each other in an effort to interpret the Bible in such a way as to demand assent to the largest number of statements having the least degree of credibility. If one of them claims that it is part of the Christian Gospel that Jonah was literally swallowed by the big fish, then the other will insist, "If the Bible reported that Jonah swallowed the big fish, I would most certainly believe that, too." "Anything you believe I believe better" becomes the contest, and the good work which saves human beings is not charity or humility but simply the sacrifice of the intellect.

It is the resulting excommunication of reason which is described in Theme 2 of the Hartford Appeal. The task which now confronts theology is to begin again to try to help the Christian community express its message in such a way that participants as well as nonparticipants in this movement can honestly say "yes" or "no" to the Christian message because they have at least some idea of what is being proclaimed.

It is not the theologian's task to devise formulae describing the Christian faith so inclusively that nobody could possibly deny them, and thus to convert the world "by definition." This is an unfair game which does violence to reason and honesty, and it is not understood as a compliment by those who, for their own good reasons, prefer not to be Christians yet suddenly find themselves included "by definition." One could escape the forced conversion "by inquisition" by dying at the stake; the forced conversion "by definition" is simply inescapable. Thus terms like "anonymous Christians" should be used sparingly if at all.

Neither is it the task of the theologian to devise formulae describing the Christian faith which are so exclusive that anybody with a shred of intellectual integrity and historical information must reject them immediately, since they demand the abject surrender of his God-given reason, not to God but to the authors of these unhappy formulations.

In the task of defining the Christian message for our time, clergy as well as academic spokesmen for the Christian Faith should avoid standing in awe of what is called "modern thought" as if it could supply not only tools for the understandable expression of the Christian message, which it can, but also the final criteria for judging the validity of this message, which it cannot. At the same time they should take seriously the wealth of the Christian tradition inherited from the past, without attempting to repristinate the allegedly perfect theological vision of one period or the other.

The eschatological orientation of the Christian movement should protect theologians from illusions concerning the superiority or finality of any period of *human* history, past, present, or future. This same orientation should, however, inspire hope that human communication is possible and, while we hold this treasure of the Gospel in earthen vessels, we hold, indeed, a treasure which may be so perceived by others if we do not let the earthen vessels obstruct the view. And while we may see the truth only dimly as in a very old-fashioned mirror, there is a truth to be seen which all the distortions of the inadequate mirror cannot ultimately obscure. This vision can and must be shared. It is the reality of this treasure and vision which is at stake whenever the attempt is being made to reduce theology to anthropology. This is the reason why the notion that "religious language refers to human experience and nothing else" must be categorically rejected. Similarly, the preoccupation with subjective religious feelings, and the various efforts at manipulating the supernatural carried on inside and outside of the Christian churches, which has become so popular, should be seen as idolatrous. Far from being hailed as harbingers of religious revival, they should be recognized as opposed to the God who spoke and it was, "and the Word [which] became flesh and dwelt among us, full of grace and *truth.*"

Obsessed by Relevance

If an uneasy relationship, if not enmity, to reason and reasonable discourse is one problem which plagues contemporary Protestantism; a second, no less serious, is the almost obsessive quest for relevance. Again, it could be claimed that "concern for the matter at hand," which may be a definition of relevance, motivated the Reformers of the sixteenth century. In whatever manner Luther's *Ninety-five Theses* were distributed, they dealt with a matter of considerable current interest; otherwise their incredibly rapid spread across Europe would be hard to explain. It is true that nothing of general interest in the sixteenth century escaped the attention of the Reformers. Both Luther and Calvin made not very insightful observations regarding the new theories of Copernicus about the arrangement of the heavenly bodies, for example. On most important matters they commented at length. Luther's *Address to the Christian Nobility* was an obvious effort to speak to the issues which troubled his fellow citizens at the time. Calvin's relevance to Geneva was so evident that the council of this city had to ask him back because, in their judgment, the city could not operate successfully without his leadership. It was Calvin's relevance to the solution of the problems of Geneva which led to the successful effort to urge him to return. But Calvin *was* relevant to the problems of Geneva; he was not simply trying to find some issue that would make him *appear* to be relevant.

This is the difference between the relevance of a Luther and Calvin to the central issues of their age and the frantic quest for relevance of contemporary Protestantism. A number of themes of the Hartford Appeal attempt to describe this quest. "Jesus can only be understood in terms of contemporary models of humanity." Or, "The world must set the agenda for the Church. Social, political, and economic programs to improve the quality of life are ultimately normative for the Church's mission in the world."

Again it might appear that the problem is here addressed in

its liberal expression. But the effort to make Jesus into a political agitator of the left, like the *Comrade Jesus* of the late Sarah Cleghorn and all the succeeding attempts to see him as an early version of Ernesto "Che" Guevara, so popular in certain circles, are equaled in intensity by the even more bizarre attempts to make him the prototype of the successful businessman and the inspiration for the victorious defense of capitalism against socialism and communism. Here Bruce Barton's book *The Man Nobody Knows* must stand as the classical example of Jesus' alleged capitalist relevance.

The agenda is set by the world. And what is the agenda? For Americans it is often "the religion of the Republic," appropriately enshrined on our money: "In God We Trust," *"Novus Ordo Seclorum," "Annuit coeptis."* The inscriptions on the dollar bill supply the catechism and politicians write the commentary:

Ours is the most advanced, most productive, richest, and most powerful society that humanity has seen since the dawn of history. What were the key elements in the formula we have followed which allowed us—in the brief span of two centuries—to raise up on this continent a nation which is a model for the world and a credit to mankind? It was freedom—freedom to work and to worship—to learn—to choose—to fashion the best life attainable with individual initiative, imagination, and courage. It was an unfettered free enterprise economic system that delivered to each man and woman the rewards they earned.[2]

With this sort of drivel as the agenda, it becomes the task of religion to maintain the illusion. For that large part of the world scared to death by the changes that are occurring, the Church and its Jesus are devices to tell the earth to stop turning and to guarantee that the status quo is frozen forever. It is fascinating to observe Protestant sectarians who are unwilling to pray the Lord's Prayer with anybody who does not assent to their sectarian vision suddenly embrace everybody in the common cause of defending capitalism and what they like to call the "American Way of Life." Thus J. A. O. Preus, the fundamentalist leader of the right wing of The Lutheran Church—Missouri Synod, and author of their official key to the Scriptures, preached at the command performance chapel services in the Nixon White House. His entire effort, which apparently attempts to restore his denomination to its nineteenth-century position, is actually a cover-up for a strange utilization of the language of nineteenth-century conservative Lutheranism in order to endorse a peculiarly reactionary variety of American culture religion.

But while the advocates of relevance on the right see the world's agenda as demanding a holding action by the Church —even if this means "presenting arms" and using military force to stop the changes taking place in Asia, Africa, Latin America, and the United States—the advocates of relevance on the left endorse all revolutions and see every change as God's hand at work in the affairs of humanity. Here the agenda of the world suggests that religion endorse any and all leftist revolutions. Thus while the repression of a black majority by a white minority in Namibia is seen for what it is, hardly a word is said about Uganda and the efforts to exterminate a black majority by a black minority. OPEC oil sheiks become forces of liberation and democracy against "fascist" Israel, and following the world's agenda means to supply religious justification to whatever human beings happen to want at the moment. Nobody has presented this theology of "radical chic" more persuasively than Harvey Cox in a succession of books that have in common only a charming style and the effort to keep up with the rapidly changing agenda of the world. Nobody has criticized this approach more incisively than Jacques Ellul, who wrote in 1972 about one of Cox's books:

The latest fabulous example of justification is Harvey Cox's celebrated book, *The Secular City.* It is hard to believe that a book so feebly thought through, so loaded with historical error, so sociologically and theologically superficial, so ordinary, with its repetition of all the commonplaces about secularization and the profane, and lacking in any depth in the subject, that a book so dubious in its historical analyses and so generalized in its sociology—that such a book would enjoy such a success. Just one thing explains it: It offers the public a justification for what is going on in the world, for what man is in the process of doing. It is true that modern man in his most fallen aspect wants exactly above everything else that someone should come along to tell him that he is right in doing what he is doing. That was the springboard for all the propaganda. From the standpoint of ideology and publicity, *The Secular City* is a great book. It supplies precisely the "solemn complement" (that Marx rightly accuses religion of supplying). Urban anonymity? That is great. That is freedom. Urban mobility is admirable, the very condition of progress. Pragmatism conforms to God's way of acting. The profane accords with God's will. The secular city is the meeting place of man and God. Since man's technological power is constantly increasing, the Church's message consists in giving assurance that it is up to man to create his own destiny.

This is a tissue of commonplaces, all of which are entirely nonbiblical and are rooted in an *imaginary* factor in modern society. Here is where theology does indeed become a completely futile superstructure. Yet, as Marx rightly said time and again, no matter how futile and tasteless it might be, it nevertheless turns into a deadly poison, in that it prevents man from seeing things as they really are. It causes him to live an illusion and to turn his back on the real. *The Secular City* is the prime example, for our modern society, of the opiate of the people.[3]

It is this manner of following the agenda of the world, whether done by J. A. O. Preus or Harvey Cox, which the Hartford Appeal calls into question, especially when this effort at relevance defends the violence of undeclared wars or senseless revolutions. In a quest for relevance, preachers do not only present arms to the forces of the status quo but also to the often equally violent and destructive "rebels without a cause."

The Christian faith could act as one of the most powerful de-alienating forces if theologians would only abandon their obsession with a fraudulent relevance. But in order to do so, and to help people to "see things as they are," it must be proclaimed in such a way as to reveal the illusions of the right, about capitalism and the American Way of Life, with the same honesty as the illusions of the left, with their glorification of revolution and utopian expectations. It can do so only if it resists the efforts from both directions to co-opt Jesus, the Christ, into the ideologies of the right or the left. The best way to achieve this is to take seriously the authority of Jesus as the eternal word and the presence of God with us. This New Testament Jesus is hard to fit into the programs of the right or the left, of the advocates of salvation by some nostalgic faith in the past or some euphoric faith in the future. It is the Gospel's concern with the ambiguity of the existence of women and men in their present predicaments which must be emphasized. Human beings who have to live in a world in which good and evil are strangely mixed in their environment and in each human heart must not be sacrificed either to the perfectionist illusions of an imaginary past or the equally per-fectionist illusions about an imaginary future. We have to live now in the midst of a world in which the saving message for me may well be: "Let him who is without sin cast the first stone." Our task is not to point to our glorious history and our past accomplishments or to an elusive future which we cannot foresee, but to try now to live courageously in spite of all the ambiguities of saints and sinners in which we fully share. When Jesus was confronted by the doubting disciples of John the Baptist he sent this message to John, "Go and tell John what you have seen and heard: the blind receive their sight, the lame walk, lepers are cleansed, and the deaf hear, the dead are raised up, the poor have good news preached to them. And blessed is he who takes no offense at me" (Luke 7:22,23).

In some small way we may be empowered to share in these signs of God's coming kingdom if we find ways to sustain human beings in their life together now. All human answers to the problems of this world are penultimate. God's ultimate answer will be a surprise to believers and unbelievers alike; in the meantime we are allowed to care for each other, show concern for each human being. In the abstract ideologies of both the right and the left, human persons count for very little; only the ultimate outcome matters and the end justifies any means which allegedly will help achieve it. A truly Christian relevance means concern and action in order to prevent people from being sacrificed to abstractions, be they those of the free enterprise system, dialectical materialism, machismo, women's liberation, or whatever the current fashion demands. "The Sabbath was made for human beings and not human beings for the Sabbath" is the verdict over the ideologies which have so successfully co-opted the Christian movement. "The norms for the Church's activity derive from its own perception of God's will for the world."

The Scandal of Being Radical

If relevance and following the agenda set by the world is not the answer, does this not undercut the radical character of the Christian Gospel? Is not the emphasis on Jesus as the Christ, and on the biblical witness concerning him, an escape from the involvement in the world which the cross of Christ demonstrates and symbolizes? As Theme 11 formulates this claim: "An emphasis on God's transcendence is at least a hindrance to, and perhaps incompatible with, Christian concern and action."

What, indeed, is radical Christianity? Is it really the reductionism which tries to trim from the biblical witness all those elements that are not plausible to the "cultured despisers of religion"? Is it radical to say things in a way that will not give offense? To eliminate from your message all controversial elements so that you may sound like any other moderately educated person? Nothing has been less radically Christian than the attempts on the part of some Protestant theologians to sound like well-meaning supporters of the "conventional wisdom" that prevails at the university faculty club. This is no better than the effort on the part of others to sound just like every racist, sexist, or chauvinistic flag-waver. Is it radical Christianity to proclaim geological opinions about the age of the earth or the extent of Noah's flood as the mark of true orthodoxy? Such obsession with trivialities can hardly be classified as defense of the faith. Indeed, there are different conventional wisdoms that one can conform to. But conformity to the conventional wisdom of your subculture is not radicalism. The opposition to the culture religion of one group from the vantage point of the culture religion of another group does not help us to escape from the falsification of the Gospel by culture religion. Both the right and the left glorify a culture which is radically challenged by the New Testament and the proclamation of Jesus as the Christ.

The Hartford Appeal points toward the radical (in the sense of root) assertion of the Christian movement in its last theme, where it rejects the claim that "the question of hope beyond death is irrelevant or at best marginal to the Christian understanding of human fulfillment." In a death-obsessed age (in recent years the most popular religion courses in American colleges and universities have dealt with death and dying), an age when the finality of death is the certainty which supplies the somber background to Western thought, both capitalist and Marxist, the radical Christian assertion of the ultimate triumph of the God of Abraham, Isaac, and Jacob, who has chosen to be a God of the living and not of the dead, is revolutionary.

It was always thus. As long as Paul discussed religion and morality at Athens everybody had a good time. When he asserted the resurrection of the dead, the mood changed: "Some mocked; but others said, 'We will hear you again about this.'" Don't call us. We'll call you.

Yet it is this insistence on the victory of life which gave the Christian movement the power to transvalue all values in the first century. Political powers whose final weapon was the ability to kill their opponents did not know what to do with people who believed that God had said "yes" to life in the paradigmatic death and resurrection of Jesus, the Christ.

This notion was as offensive at the end of the first century as it is at the end of the twentieth. It was radical. And it was a scandal then as it is a scandal now. Yet there is not much point in talking about the Christian faith without coming to terms with this scandal of the cross and the resurrection. All the moralistic legalism of the defenders of the status quo or the champions of revolution and utopia has little to do with the New Testament proclamation of God's victory over the last enemy.

We live in an age of joyless hedonism. The political movements of the right and the left vie with each other in an effort to supply the greatest good for the greatest number and seem like rival deck stewards competing with each other about the arrangement of the deck chairs just before the Titanic hits the iceberg. The general awareness of this situation is the reason why our hedonism is so joyless. For Christians to get into this act of the deck stewards and to come up with an alternative arrangement seems ludicrous in view of the radical news which constitutes the Gospel and which, if true, changes the human situation completely. It is quoted at the end of the Hartford Appeal. It is the articulation and application of this truly radical insight which is the task of Christians. Everything else is ultimately trivial. "We believe that God raised Jesus from the dead and are '. . . convinced that there is nothing in death or life, in the realm of spirits or superhuman powers, in the world as it is or in the world as it shall be, in the forces of the universe, in heights or depths—nothing in all creation that can separate us from the love of God in Christ Jesus our Lord.' " (Theme 13)

A radical Christian theology for our time can be derived from this Gospel, but only by people who believe it and take it seriously. In contemporary Protestantism the people on the right seem to believe this Gospel but fail to take it seriously; otherwise they could not be so preoccupied by what they call "fundamentals" as to obscure the proclamation of God's victory for humankind by their legalistic and literalistic controversies.

The people on the left may indeed take this Gospel seriously, but precisely for this reason they do not believe it. That is why they substitute human fulfillment, self-realization, and evolution (not as a biological theory but as a means of grace) for the radical Gospel. The Hartford Appeal would seem to be a call to the radical center of the Christian proclamation, the *kerygma* of the New Testament.

By doing this it transcends all denominational boundaries. After all, it is an appeal issued by Orthodox, Roman Catholic, and Protestant Christians. Thus it demonstrates that ecumenism has come a long way. No longer do Christians have to be content with an occasional ecumenical meeting. They may now be able to do theology together, addressing common problems and attacking jointly the dangers they perceive. Even the fact that those who publicly expressed their disapproval of the Hartford Appeal came from various denominational camps, both Roman Catholic and Protestant, is an indication that the point may have been reached where theological issues can be discussed without any narrow denominational uniformity. This, too, may contribute to a truly radical Christian theology. Perhaps the Hartford Appeal has been one modest step in this direction.

Notes

1. Cf. Wilhelm Link, *Das Ringen Luthers um die Freiheit der Theologie von der Philosophie,* München, 1940.

2. Senator James O. Eastland, as quoted in Arthur Herzog, *The B.S. Factor, The Theory and Technique of Faking in America,* New York: Penguin Books (1974), p. 31.

3. Jacques Ellul, *Hope in a Time of Abandonment,* New York: Seabury Press (1973), p. 152 f.

Hartford and the Future
of Roman Catholic Thought

A Creative Alienation

CARL J. PETER

It is rather commonplace to hear or read descriptions of the very different ways in which Christian faith is thought about and practiced by Roman Catholics in the United States at present. Mary Perkins Ryan, to take one example, has called attention to three distinct types of Catholics and has designated them respectively as *preconciliar, conciliar* (Vatican II), and *developing.* They correspond to three outlooks manifested by Catholics in attempts to answer the question: "Why get up in the morning?" The preconciliar type sees very little of daily life as affording real contact with God, whom one meets in holy things and places or confronts when there is question of temptation and sin. A person rises from bed in the morning to be about the most important task of all—soul-saving for self and others. The second type regards the purpose of life as one of responding to God's love in the midst of the Christian community; directly by prayer and worship and indirectly by one's daily work. Finally, for the developing Catholic, God is to be found in the midst of human experience and is to be served above all else by serving people.[1] The differences between the three types are obvious, but even in the title of her book Mary

Perkins Ryan points to a fact that she clearly wants others in her church to reflect on: *We Are All in This Together.* A large number of Catholics are indeed still in the same church in this country despite the remarkably different ways in which they assess and evaluate their faith in relation to getting out of bed instead of staying there all day long.

The Church of Your Choice

One result of such coexistence is a church of shoppers affected by religious consumerism. The latter shows itself, for example, in the way many Catholics search out the type of worship they prefer with much less concern for shoe leather, gasoline, time, or parish boundaries than would have been the case not so long ago. This is true whether their preference be for the Latin rather than English mass, for dialogue homily, for consciousness raising, or for liturgical dance. Not a few shopping Catholics regard their confessional affiliation as important enough to search out a congenial pastor, a sympathetic curate, a competent religious education director, a wise moral counselor, or a prayer group where they feel comfortable even if definite inconvenience is involved. How many shoppers there are and, even more, how long they will stick to their shopping, is uncertain. That they are not a figment of anyone's imagination is beyond doubt. They are at least a symptom of what is meant when one speaks of polarization in the Roman Catholic Church. Such a church has members who are fairly sure they know what they need religiously and, as a result, what they want. But they often differ radically one from another when it comes to saying precisely what it is they think they need and therefore expect from their local church community in the persons of its leaders and other members.

To be sure this is not a peculiarly Roman Catholic phenomenon. However, because the practice of religious consumerism differs so from what was popularly expected of Roman Catholics in the past, not a few observers seem inclined to think that it may be especially significant when found among members of that church today. Whether or not this is true, Roman Catholicism surely does have its factions setting social action over against preaching the Gospel and in dispute over liturgical experimentation; as well as attitudes toward women's rights, war and peace, racial discrimination, sex education, catechetics, and ecumenism.

But it is not simply with regard to forms of prayer and worship or over moral attitudes that Catholics in the United States find themselves divided. One can, another observer has maintained, find three groups of Catholics who relate quite differently to belief itself and, as a result, to one another. There are, Gabriel Moran wrote in 1972, in the middle generation of American Catholics many who no longer believe anything.[2]

Those who are, roughly speaking, between twenty-five and forty-five years of age were taught to accept Roman Catholic dogmas as true, and did in fact believe them. Many do so no longer. A younger age group was not trained catechetically to regard faith in the same way. They, too, do not at times accept the truth claims made by their church, but they fail to have the anxiety experienced by the middle generation when they find they cannot believe any longer what they used to believe with little difficulty. Those who are older—with due allowance for exceptions—simply do not react either way. They still accept the old dogmas and think believing necessarily involves so doing.[3]

As to the Catholics said to be in that middle generation, one simply cannot deny that they are to be found in parishes throughout the country. Their problems at times also affect those younger than twenty-five and older than forty-five. Perhaps, too, a fair number in that middle group have not changed nearly to this extent and may even be in danger of becoming disaffected from their church because of a widespread malaise caused by tensions they do not experience personally. But very many seem to have changed every bit as much Moran has said.

From another point of view, Langdon Gilkey has described the shifts taking place within Catholicism as a result of a confrontation with modernity.[4] A crisis has resulted from the impact secular culture and thought have had on a faith that until fifteen years ago had largely immunized itself from the doubts and denials stemming from the spirit of the Enlightenment. Catholic conservatives wish to reverse that impact while radicals have more or less distanced themselves from the doctrinal dimension of their church. Gilkey sees the Catholic liberals as distinct from both these groups. They recognize the need for change and are attempting to bring Christian faith in the Roman Catholic tradition into a mutually advantageous give-and-take with contemporary secular culture.

Profound disillusionment has occasioned yet another description of the present state of Catholic faith and practice. James Hitchcock has written of what he calls "the decline and fall of radical Catholicism." He is of the conviction that despite the hopes of Vatican II, the all-pervasive spiritual revival that was expected did not take place. Efforts to reform the church have caused more harm than good; renewal—to use the term so often associated with updating or *aggiornamento*—has obviously been a failure.[5] Those Catholics who most wanted their church to change have found themselves becoming increasingly embittered because of delays and the frustration of reforms, but also because what they thought they wanted, even when it did come, has failed to bring the peace they anticipated. Interestingly enough Hitchcock concluded his book in 1971 by listing what he termed twenty-six heretical notions characterizing radical Catholicism.[6]

It would, to be sure, be very difficult to put together a composite picture of Roman Catholicism in the United States from the sketches given above. The authors cited are by no means all those who have taken a hand in the task. Nor do they all agree as to the causes and remedies called for by the present situation. None of them pretends to offer a definitive analysis. They were chosen because though different they have much to say that strikes home as true, and because future historians will likely have to incorporate points made by each when they set out to write their accounts of what happened to the Roman Catholic Church in the United States during the past fifteen years. It is to that church with all its present tensions that five of the original signers of the Hartford Appeal for Theological Affirmation belonged. And it is to relate that Appeal to the state of thought in that same church that this paper will primarily direct itself.

A Preliminary Assessment

For not a few Catholics in the United States, the Hartford Appeal for Theological Affirmation functioned like a symbol. Its imagery (for example, Theme 3: *"God invented us."*) communicated with a power beyond that normally associated with abstract thought. It evoked reactions of acceptance or hostility that its sometimes complex idiom (for example, Explanation 4: "a reversal of the 'imitation of Christ' ") would not have seemed likely to produce. To be sure its relation to and bearing on the state of Catholic thought are impossible to assess adequately at present, especially in a brief essay. That may be feasible when more returns have come in. Still, scattered precincts have already reported, not perhaps enough to declare Hartford a winner or a loser, but significant as indicative of trends. At the very least, Hartford has made a good number of Christians stop and think. Hence there may be some value, even at this point, in an effort to survey the reactions that have come from representative American Catholics, especially those emanating from opinion-formers. The findings may suggest that Hartford has something important to say to the Catholic theological community with regard to a number of issues of present concern. It may even make that community think of those issues in a slightly different way. If so, then Hartford may well prove to be even more of a symbol in the future than it has been already.

In an unsigned editorial, *America* found the significance of the Appeal in the weight of the signers' testimony to a commonly held core of Christian beliefs. If, it continued, the resulting challenge is picked up, ecumenical theology will be well on its way to establishing its own agenda for the next decade.[7]

Commonweal was taken by what the Appeal did not purport to be; namely, a new creed, a denunciation of individual adversaries, or a theological endeavor to deal with the doctrinal questions raised by its themes and explanations. As to the signers, they were described as a group of moderate-liberal religious leaders whose convictions have led to a document that is a retreat neither from creative theology nor from political action. On the other hand, notice has been served by Hartford that the Church is not just a joiner but must be a judge as well with regard to an increasingly materialistic and selfish dominant culture.[8]

The National Catholic Reporter carried a story which among other things was concerned with satisfying the curiosity of those wondering about the targets of the Appeal. The reader was told that as for determining who is holding, preaching, or teaching these false themes, the participants insist they had no individuals or groups in mind.[9] In a later editorial the signers of the Appeal, who are described as centrist rather than conservative or middle-of-the-road, are said to have succeeded in asking the right questions. Their help is then sought in the task of finding the right answers and making the progress that conservatives of the future will fight to protect.[10]

The Wanderer gave its readers Elliot Wright's account of the Appeal and the events leading to the latter's publication.[11] Dr. Ralph McInerny of Notre Dame was quoted as saying that the statement should be applied to the drafters as well as any other audience. This comment may be of help to many who were and are perplexed as to the meaning of Hartford. If, in words attributed to yet another signer, the Appeal intended to say "Go and sin no more," giving such an admonition could be self-referential and probably was just that in the minds of a number of signers.[12]

Writing in *Twin Circle*, Archbishop Robert J. Dwyer put the Hartford Appeal in a very different literary genre than had *Commonweal*. He described it as a modern syllabus of errors but noted that its contents did not qualify as a rounded exposition of all the false and misleading trends in contemporary theological speculation. More specifically—and the Protestant-Orthodox signers may sigh with relief at this—it lacks, he said, the completeness and finality of Pope Paul's magnificant *Credo* of June 30, 1968. Asserting that the signers affirmed the groundwork of an apologetic, he thought the whole venture was positive and reassuring. Still he ended with a cautionary note. He was not sure what American Catholic theologians would do if asked to come up with a similar statement. He was pleased, however, that the Catholics who signed have held on to at least these essentials.[13]

In a column in *The National Catholic Register*, Msgr. R. G. Peters cited the remarks of *Commonweal* with a little surprise. He admitted to wondering whether the Hartford spirit may not in fact become a bandwagon with all sorts jumping aboard.[14]

An unsigned editorial in *The Long Island Catholic* called the Appeal a blow for balanced theology. It went further, however, and named offenders: at least some of the signers had in mind theologians like Harvey Cox, Juan Luis Segundo, and Gabriel Moran.[15] Here one should recall that the *Appeal* mentioned no names. Perhaps, however, one of the reasons why it was warily received by a number of Catholics was the fact that names were indeed cited in *Time* magazine's account of the meeting that produced it.[16]

The reactions of Father Andrew Greeley are noteworthy given the fact that among other qualifications he is a forthright commentator on religious news and an avid church watcher. In a column of March 6 in *The Tablet Magazine*, he wrote that the Hartford theses mark the end of romantic radicalism in

American Protestantism. He added that, characteristically, just as their separated brothers abandon it, Catholics embrace it with enthusiasm.[17]

Other Catholics writing in the religious press also took note of Hartford.[18] Those cited above should offer at least the beginning of a view of the initial reactions by those who would probably not object to being described as reporters, journalists, and religious news commentators. Theologians reacted as well and will be treated later. But what can be said by way of a summary of the positions taken by other Catholics in the religious press? They were surprised almost to a person. Most were made to think—both those who are popularly thought of as conservatives and those regarded as liberals in the polarized Catholicism described in the first section of this essay. They found the drafters in general hard to categorize. The Catholic signers in particular are referred to as fellow liberals or as moderates, not as conservatives.[19]

The document itself is said to be timely and thought-provoking. Like a parable, it was seen to be open-ended and to leave application to be made by others—not in the thundering anathemas that were often hurled vaguely in the direction of unnamed opponents by churches in the past, but in language calculated to make the reader ask "Is it I, Lord?" In not a few cases it was noted that Hartford might be a beginning: as a statement of faith-convictions regarded as central, however unpopular they might be in the estimation of the prevailing culture. But could the signers of Hartford do any more to promote a dialogue with those who for one reason or another could not accept the style and/or content of the Appeal? This question was also asked. An affirmative answer would suggest that the Appeal offers a possible opening to the future. At the very least it has already struck a responsive chord in the hearts of many Catholics. The attention given to it in newspapers representing the entire spectrum of theological outlook in Roman Catholicism in this country has been one of guarded sympathy. It remains to be seen whether the interest manifested thus far is real or of the type that says "We will hear more of you another time."

Unavoidable Issues

At this point, an effort to assess a number of critical reactions on the part of American Catholic theologians who did not take part in the Hartford deliberations is imperative. Otherwise the relation of the Appeal to the present state of Catholic thought will be treated even more inadequately than is at any rate inevitable, given the vastness of the topic.

One of the most interesting references to Hartford is that of Brother Luke Salm in his presidential address closing the 1975 convention of the Catholic Theological Society of America.[20] He is one who has worked quietly and effectively for long years to open the doors and windows of the society in question. He has helped it become less foreign to the American academic scene, less clerical, and less male. With such a background, he was in a unique position to assess the thirty previous years of the existence of the society. He did so in a masterful and delightful fashion. As to the society's present condition, he noted that he did not think it should regard the errors mentioned in the Hartford Appeal as threats to the society itself. It was rather the isolation of Catholic theology from the world of politics, economics, and social action that he felt to be a more serious danger. He added that the Appeal was too reminiscent of the generalizations that characterized Roman pronouncements in the past.[21]

Despite the long experience of Luke Salm with the endeavors of this professional society of Catholic theologians, matters may not be as clear cut as he thinks. Their common effort to remove unwarranted ecclesiastical interference from the theological enterprise does not excuse Catholic theologians from the academic obligation of criticizing one another more than they have in the recent past. If a colleague short-circuits critical inquiry by an appeal to faith, others should call him or her to task. They have not always done so, or even been allowed to. Today, however, the situation is somewhat changed. If the method of hard-headed inquiry into the meaning and truth of the Christian mystery obscures, misplaces, or even seems to do away with the mystery itself, then, not merely in the name of faith but in that of scientific fidelity, this should be pointed out. There are good reasons to hold that every Christian theologian worth his or her salt must run the risk of failing to give critical thought its due or of making the nondivine the adequate measure of mystery. The past history of the Catholic Theological Society of America has not confirmed its present members in grace sufficiently to assure their conquering the second of these temptations. Hence Hartford has every reason to be taken seriously by the members of that society precisely because they have come to regard their function of dissent and criticism more seriously than did some of their predecessors. Failure to acknowledge the divine as mysterious, however much such an affirmation may fly in the face of the contemporary *Zeitgeist*, is a temptation Hartford should call to the attention of many; even of Roman Catholic theologians after Vatican II.

Richard P. McBrien of Boston College also reacted to Hartford.[22] He wrote that its initial intent was to take aim at the left wing of contemporary Christianity, and that according to reports Avery Dulles urged his fellow conferees to consider the excesses of the right. To set the record straight on that, there was from the beginning of the Hartford meeting a general desire to criticize the misplacement of transcendence whether by the right or by the left. To single out one individual as responsible for this attempt at evenhandedness is fair neither to that individual nor to the group. Early in the Hartford discussions, two of the participants made available to their colleagues a list of antitheses that were intended to clarify the meaning of the original theses or propositions that had been prepared for the consideration of the group of eventual signers. Others felt this need no less keenly and were no less determined to avoid giving ammunition to any who, in the name of respecting Christian tradition, exploit it uncritically by seeking in it ready-made answers and solutions to today's questions and problems. It simply cannot be said that those who planned the Hartford meeting expected the participants to assemble and ratify propositions already drafted against the theological left wing. Nor did any individual or pair of individuals bring the conference to face the abuses of the far right theologically, as if their colleagues were otherwise unaware of a need to do so. But McBrien also took the explanations given in the Appeal and argued that one could redraft the latter from them solely. The result would, he maintained, be a very different picture of contemporary Christian theology and the conferees.[23] It is true that one could indeed do what McBrien says. But what would that accomplish? One could also—and some have—recast Vatican II's Constitution on the Church making Chapter III (dealing with the hierarchy) either peripheral or the very heart of the document. The results would not and do not tell what church and world the participants of Vatican II were speaking of. Nor does a recasting of Hartford on the sole basis of the explanations.

The spirit of Gabriel Moran's reply is caught well in its title: "On Not Asking the Right Questions."[24] He would not wish to defend any one of the thirteen themes as stated but feels that preaching the same "churchy" language that has already been found wanting is not an adequate response to them either. Hartford does just that. Moran criticizes it for failing to distinguish theological from religious statements and the modern meaning of church from other possible forms of religious institutions. He thinks the Appeal cannot even ask the question whether religious statements stemming from Christian history may be made by people who do not accept the premises of Christian theology. Moran may well have read more into the Appeal than is there or than is warranted by the traditional "churchy" terms that do appear. He has, however, centered in on the relation of Christian theology to Christian faith or commitment. Hartford may yet help contemporary Roman Catholic theologians face this important question more adequately and in a more sustained fashion than they have heretofore.[25]

Gregory Baum regards the Appeal as theologically quite unsatisfactory.[26] It contains a curious and untraditional separation of transcendence and immanence while at the same time failing to recognize the human as a locus of the divine. He agrees that it is important to safeguard the sense of divine transcendence. What is more, the view of God's presence operative in the humanization of the world should not lead to a Christianity that has identified itself with the dominant cultural trends of its age. But Hartford, Baum thinks, does not meet either concern; it lacks language that confirms and clarifies commitment as a source of critique, liberation, and life.[27]

It may not be amiss to offer two brief observations in reply to this criticism. It is, George Tavard says quite rightly, a truism that an assertion of divine transcendence (like that made at Hartford) may underestimate divine immanence.[28] But a further word seems called for, this time by way of question. Baum knows no theologian who holds the thirteen themes. But one has every reason to ask: Are the theological implications of the rejection of those themes important enough to spell out? Perhaps in dialogue he could try to help the Hartford signers find a way to affirm the transcendence of God without endangering divine immanence or, on the other hand, appearing to make the nondivine the adequate measure of mystery. The very attempt could hardly fail to come to grips with the question of how and under what conditions the human is a locus of the divine.

In a typically gentlemanly response, David Tracy conceded that the Appeal has stirred up authentic theological discussion better than any document of recent years.[29] His disagreement lies in the fact that it is based on a mistaken notion of the role of the theologian and of theology. Churches, however constituted in terms of specific polity and order, ought to proclaim affirmations and negations (beliefs), but theologians as such should not. Hartford fails to make this distinction, and the confusion of roles has perhaps unwittingly given aid and comfort to the theological right. What is more, Theme 13, which deals with the question of hope beyond death, is either so unclear as to be itself debilitating or so clear as to preclude further discussion. It may be worthwhile to look at this contention a bit more closely.

Tracy argues that it is the role of a theologian as such to deal with the evidence, mode of argumentation, and grounds that any other theologian puts forward to back his or her specific conclusions. Theologians should, in other words, criticize one another with regard to the way they reach conclusions. But are not Theme 13 of Hartford and its accompanying explanation patient of an interpretation that has them do that at least implicitly? The ensemble on this view would say that those Christian theologians, for example, who are unconcerned about failing to get around to dealing with the question of hope beyond death, fail to do justice to the data they are to interpret and criticize. The conclusion that their omission is unimportant is unwarranted; they should be worried about that omission. If this message is a tautology, as Tracy seems to say, it is one that may nevertheless have something to say to not a few who reflect on and write of Christianity today.

But what of those theologians who do consider the question of hope beyond death, and who give other than traditional answers to it? Hartford may well be interpreted as an affirmation that, in this case as well, the way their conclusion has been reached does not seem to do justice to the data to be interpreted: for example, Saint Paul and First Corinthians. To them Hartford would be saying that such an answer may in fact not be a conclusion at all (or at least not one that is warranted), but rather a premise that is somewhat arbitrary despite arguments made on its behalf. In this sense, proclaiming an affirmation might very well be an appropriate public stance of a theologian wishing to call attention to assumptions which, despite reflection and argumentation, remain only assumptions.

Which propositions do and which do not call for affirmation by the Christian is a matter this writer would prefer to see theologians try to help determine instead of simply leaving the task to the churches. Where would the churches, whatever their structures, look to get the answers as to what affirmations are required for the Christian confession? This signer of the Appeal would like to think the churches should have recourse to prayer and study, and therefore turn not least or last of all to theologians—surely for the study and hopefully at times for the prayer as well. But beliefs and their relation to theologizing are a matter that will be referred to in the final section of this essay.

In short, prominent Catholic theologians reacting to Hartford have viewed it with surprise, wondered who its targets might be, and admitted that its appeal for affirming transcendence is not hysteria. They have, however, hesitated to describe the concern underlying that appeal as one that should grip the theologian either as such or at least in the way it did the signers. The reaction of those who thought the right wing was being unwittingly aided by Hartford was surprisingly mild. By and large, the Appeal was seen as leaving a good bit to be desired in what it did not say and in the way it said what it did. Here again, as in the case of the journalists and religious news commentators, opinion-formers have been cited because they reveal not a little about the state of Catholic thought in the United States and Canada. For them, too, Hartford functioned rather like a symbol.

To summarize, reactions of the Catholic press have been remarkably positive with regard to the Hartford Appeal, this despite badly divided Catholic readership throughout the country. Roman Catholic theologians for their part—especially those who have reacted critically—have pointed to issues that Hartford, to its credit or discredit as one may think, makes unavoidable; namely, how to assert transcendence without diminishing divine presence in the world and history, and how faith (especially beliefs) should relate to theology and church. To be sure, the religious press and the reactions of a number of theologians hardly give an adequate picture of Hartford's relation to the present state of Catholic thought. They do, however, offer a preliminary assessment. And perhaps they do more as well.

Setting the Agenda

One of the Hartford contentions that upset not a few was the rejection of the theme that the world must set the agenda for the Church (Theme 10). One may now ask, especially after the criticisms, whether Hartford may have a role to play in helping set the agenda for Catholic theologizing over the next few years. An affirmative answer seems warranted. What Hartford has already done, even in the opinion of its critics, is to generate much discussion of divine transcendence. It may have even more to contribute. A number of areas where its very existence may prove beneficial will now be indicated.

It is well-known that during the past decade one of the factors involved in the polarization of the Roman Catholic Church in the United States is the dissent of many of its members from its official teaching on a wide variety of matters. To be sure, a real, if limited, acknowledgement of the right to such dissent under certain conditions was made in a pastoral letter of the National Conference of Catholic Bishops during the troubled year of 1968.[30] Still there remains at present widespread unwillingness to face up officially to the fact of such dissent and, even more, an understandable difficulty in learning how to cope with its implications in church planning. On the theological scene the dispute regarding dissent is reflected in (though it is by no means identical with) that regarding the infallibility of the church's teaching office. Now, neither the practical resolution of the difficulty regarding the conditions and limits of loyal dissent, nor the more theoretical resolution of the debate among Catholics regarding infallibility, is in sight.[31] Without stretching the evidence it is probably true to say that, among themselves, the Roman Catholic signers of Hartford would mirror the divergencies their church is experiencing with regard to dissent, infallibility, and the rights of conscience. Yet, nevertheless, they were able to assert in common the transcendence of the Father of Jesus Christ. Indeed this consensus was significant, not least of all because of differences on issues like those just referred to.

In this way, Hartford should give the Catholic theological community reason to stop and think. Would it be possible, on a much broader spectrum than that represented by the five original Catholic signers, to produce a common confession regarding the unsurpassable importance of Jesus Christ for man's future? Such a confession could speak to a very wide audience to be sure, especially if characterized by an effort to articulate convictions in as credible and convincing a manner as possible to those not accepting Christian premises. Indeed, it might do even more. It might give flesh and blood to the otherwise increasingly dubious assertion that what Catholics believe in common as Christians is still far more significant than what divides them, however serious the disputes about infallibility and the right to dissent may yet be. Hartford has already been a sign of unity amid difference in a small part of the Catholic theological community. It might become an even more efficacious sign, but that will take more than the talents of the original signers. Clearly, however,—and it will not hurt to point this out—a combined Catholic effort to articulate reasons for taking Christian conviction seriously could hardly help but prove ecumenically helpful.

Besides posing the challenge to make more than an idle boast of unity amid theological diversity, Hartford may direct attention to another need as well. It has to do with the relation of believing Christian faith to doing Christian theology. Is such faith a *sine qua non* for the latter? Or is it simply a sociological fact that many who have done Christian theology have also accepted the core beliefs of Christian faith?[32] To his credit, a critic like David Tracy has pointed to this issue. He has also found Hartford wanting on this score. At the very least this focuses attention on the issue itself. One might, however, question Tracy's assessment. Hartford asserts that certain affirmations are called for today because their pervasive denial or absence is debilitating to the life and mission of the churches. Now one might sign the Hartford Appeal and still argue that to do Christian theology one need not have experienced Christian conversion or accept Christian beliefs. So arguing, one could still maintain that given the possibility of doing Christian theology while denying or at least not assenting to the truth claims involved in Christian beliefs, there is another, no less scientific, way of doing such theology, one which at the same time involves accepting those Christian beliefs. Hartford is patient of the interpretation that when Christian theology is done pervasively in the first manner, the churches are debilitated. Of course, it neither says nor denies this. But it seems strange that such an interpretation did not suggest itself to critics.

Perhaps some Catholic theologians, in an honest effort to win recognition of the scientific character of their discipline, insist too one-sidedly on the genuine character of Christian theology done by those who perform the appropriate investigations of the data without commitment to basic Christian beliefs. Without the one-sidedness, the position is at least debatable. But when such authors—and Tracy as recently as 1974 was one—go on to point out a sociological fact, namely, that many theologians perform those operations while at the same time accepting basic beliefs, they leave their reader hanging. Does that combination of critical rationality and believing faith have something to offer the churches and/or theology that neither component by itself can be expected to achieve? This signer answers affirmatively but admits that the work of proof is incomplete. Hartford at least provides another obvious opportunity to ask the question which has not a little to do with Catholicism's apprehensions as it confronts modernity.

The Appeal also offers Catholic theologians the chance to reconsider their theological priorities. The need for greater freedom and respect for rights within and outside their church has claimed much of their attention over the past decade. Rightly so. But in the process of continued efforts in such a direction there is a pitfall to be avoided. Christian theologians with such concerns may be too easily embarrassed at the prospect of personally holding to certain basic Christian positions that others may in all honesty feel compelled to describe as unenlightened. Despite its implicit call for rational discourse in faith, Hartford can be seen as offering a similar reminder to the effect that those who accept Christian beliefs must, at least at times, expect to feel a little ill at ease for so doing.[33]

By way of conclusion, one of the most influential groups of thinkers and planners in the world today holds officially that true understanding begins with alienation. Indeed, alienation, as they view it, can lead to an understanding conducive to future reconciliation. Perhaps Hartford can make Catholic theologians ask themselves about the merits of a somewhat similar contention; namely, that perhaps they have, in their efforts to confront modernity, overlooked the possibility that even today a promising source of theological understanding may be the admission of embarrassment arising from faith and beliefs, an embarrassment leading to critical reflection that may in turn gradually generate common grounds with those who originally took the offense which occasioned the embarrassment. If Hartford were to make Catholic theologians consider even this possibility, it would not necessarily lead back to any precritical age of blind obedience but just might give birth to a theological understanding that could be most fruitful in theory and practice.

Notes

1. Ryan, Mary Perkins, *We're All in This Together* (New York: Holt, Rinehart, and Winston, 1972), pp. 8–25.

2. Moran, Gabriel, *The Present Revelation: The Search for Religious Foundations* (New York: Herder and Herder, 1972).

3. *Ibid.*, pp. 3, 4.

4. Gilkey, Langdon, *Catholicism Confronts Modernity: A Protestant View* (New York: Seabury, 1975).

5. Hitchcock, James, *The Decline and Fall of Radical Catholicism* (New York: Herder and Herder, 1971), p. 5.

6. *Ibid.*, pp. 225–228.

7. "Ecumenical Theology at the Crossroads," *America*, Feb. 15, 1975, p. 103.

8. "God Invented Us," *Commonweal*, Feb. 14, 1975, pp. 379–380.

9. Shoemaker, Sharlene, "Theological Statement Wins Favor: Ecumenical Plea Opposes False, Superficial Ideas," *The National Catholic Reporter*, March 7, 1975, p. 5.

10. "The Conservatives," *The National Catholic Reporter*, Apr. 18, 1975, p. 8.

11. Wright, Elliot, "Diverse Group Issues Syllabus of Theological Errors," *The Wanderer*, Feb. 20, 1975, p. 7.

12. That was surely the case with the author of this paper.

13. Dwyer, Robert J., "A Modern Syllabus of Errors," *Twin Circle*, March 30, 1975, pp. 2, 15.

14. *The National Catholic Register*, March 16, 1975, p. 7.

15. "Hartford Statement Calls for Balanced Theology," *The Long Island Catholic*, Feb. 7, 1975.

16. "The Hartford Heresies," *Time*, Feb. 10, 1975, p. 47.

17. Greeley, Andrew, "Into the Swamp of Romanticism Rode the Six Hundred," *The Tablet Magazine*, March 5, 1975, p. 12.

18. At least one Catholic theologian spoke about Hartford to editors and publishers. Himself an editor *(Theological Studies)*, Father Walter Burghardt, S.J. told the Catholic Press Assn. meeting in New York on May 14 that whether they liked the Appeal or disliked it, they would not, he hoped, fail to give it further coverage. The reason he gave is that the content of Hartford represented the cutting edge of theology, indeed theology at the crossroads.

19. As noted above, *The National Catholic Reporter* said they are not conservatives while *Commonweal* described them as a group of moderate-liberal religious leaders. Jerry Filteau, writing for the National Catholic News Service, describes the Appeal's signers as having engaged in constructive criticism of fellow liberals (*The Providence Visitor*, Feb. 7, 1975, pp. 1, 10).

20. The text will be found in *The Proceedings of the Catholic Theological Society of America*, 30 (1975).

21. *Ibid.*

22. McBrien, Richard P., "A Re-View of the Hartford Themes," *The Catholic Messenger* (Davenport, Iowa), March 13, 1975, p. 8.

23. *Ibid.*

24. Moran, Gabriel, "On Not Asking the Right Questions," *Worldview*, May 1975, pp. 25–26.

25. An important exchange did take place on the theme "Is There a Catholic Theology?" at the 29th annual convention of the Catholic Theological Society of America. See *Proceedings of the C.T.S.A.* 29(1974). This hopefully was but the beginning of an ongoing discussion.

26. Baum, Gregory, "On the Human Locus of the Divine," *Worldview*, May 1975, pp. 26–27.

27. *Ibid.*

28. Tavard, George, "Locating the Divine," *Worldview*, June 1975, pp. 45–46.

29. Tracy, David, "To Be A Theologian," *Worldview*, June 1975, pp. 40–41.

30. *Human Life in Our Day* (Washington: U.S.C.C., 1968), p. 18.

31. This is true even after the exchange of letters between Hans Küng and Karl Rahner that has come to be known as their "Working Agreement to Disagree." For the text, see *America*, July 7, 1973, pp. 10–11.

32. For a very clear statement of the problem, see David Tracy's "Response to Professor Connelly" in the *Proceedings of The Catholic Theological Society of America* 29 (1974) pp. 67–77.

33. In this context it may not be amiss to mention *Humanist Manifesto II*. The latter has been described as a major social document proposing new directions for mankind, stressing belief in man and his rational powers, and criticizing theistic religion as an impediment to human development. It is a revision and updating of a manifesto issued in 1933 by thirty-four scholars, including John Dewey. Appearing in 1973, the second *Manifesto* included among other things the contention that: "As in 1933, humanists still believe that traditional theism, especially faith in the prayer-hearing God, assumed to love and care for persons, to hear and understand their prayers, and to be able to do something about them, is an unproved and outmoded faith." And again: "We find insufficient evidence for the belief in the existence of a supernatural; it is either meaningless or irrelevant to the question of the survival and fulfillment of the human race." The full text may be found in *The Humanist*, Sept.-Oct., 1973, pp. 4–9. It seems to this observer that Catholic philosophers may have taken this challenge more seriously than did theologians by and large. Cf. the reactions of Louis Dupré, *Commonweal*, Oct. 19, 1973, and his reply to the criticisms that came from three signers of the *Manifesto* (*Commonweal*, Dec. 21, 1973). See also the reaction of Dr. Jude Dougherty in *The Washington Star-News*, Sept. 2, 1973, Section F, p. 2. Perhaps the reason for the relative nonadvertence to *Humanist Manifesto II* by a number of otherwise articulate and nonreticent Catholic theologians is an unhappy experience in the first North American dialogue between Roman Catholics and humanists. Cf. John Haughey, "Humanists

Encounter a Pilgrim Church" in *America*, May 27, 1972. Of that gathering one of the signers of *Humanist Manifesto II* writes in reply to Dupré: "Professor Dupré will recall that I was as affronted as he was by the uncharitable and unjust refusal of our humanist brethren to believe in the truthfulness of our Catholic brethren at the Dialogue." Cf. *Commonweal*, Dec. 21, 1973, p. 319. It is a fact that Catholic theologians have not pursued the matter or taken up the *Manifesto* with the same lasting attention that they have given to problems in their own Church, such as family planning, sexism, rights of priests and religious dispensed from the obligations of celibacy and vows, guidelines for Catholic Health Facilities. This is not to say they had to. It is to say that Hartford may well have something to say to them, as well as it did to the author of this essay, who signed it gladly.

New Alignments

RICHARD J. MOUW

How do the concerns of the Hartford group compare with the thoughts and attitudes of "conservative-evangelicalism"? Is the Hartford document a covert (or even overt) *endorsement* of the evangelical posture? Or is it a covert (or even overt) *indictment* of many concerns associated with the evangelical position?

These may not be the most important questions to ask in assessing the Hartford phenomenon, but they are at least interesting ones. Hartford has been accused of giving aid and comfort to the theological-political "right," which in many minds places the Hartford Appeal in close proximity to evangelicalism. The fact that this is one of the few recent theological documents—perhaps the only one—that included evangelicals in a broadly ecumenical group of drafters has not gone unnoticed. Perhaps the presence of evangelicals may even have helped to kindle the suspicions of those inclined to see forces of reaction operating in the Hartford group.

While on one side the participation of evangelicals may have weakened the credibility of the Hartford group, in certain evangelical circles it seemed to have the reverse effect of weakening the credibility of the evangelical participants. In a news report on Hartford, *Christianity Today* (February 14, 1975) placed the names of Professor Smedes and myself at the top of its list of signers; having thus established our association with the Appeal, it proceeded to criticize the project in an editorial in its next issue (February 28). The Appeal, we were told, was full of "ambiguities"; worst of all, it "said nothing whatever about the problem of religious authority." (According to reliable reports, the most time-consuming discussion in the drafting of the Lausanne Covenant at the 1974 International Congress on World Evangelization was over the wording of the paragraph on "the authority and power of the Bible." It would be interesting to see if the compromise wording agreed to at Lausanne—that the Bible is inerrant in what it "affirms"—is too "unambiguous" for acceptance on the part of most of the Hartford group.) In short, *Christianity Today*'s verdict that Hartford "has done more to raise questions than to provide answers" clearly implied that the project was unworthy of evangelical participation or endorsement.

This is, in certain respects, a curious reaction to Hartford. Evangelicals may indeed wish to hear more details than the Appeal provided; they may be curious as to how their favorite questions concerning biblical inerrancy, the supernatural, and the need for personal conversion would be answered by the Hartford group. But the Hartford project is surely a step forward in creating an atmosphere wherein discussion of theological specifics can be pursued with more integrity than has been possible in recent decades. Indeed, in its fundamental thrust the Appeal locates the root difficulty at exactly the same point as one of twentieth-century evangelicalism's ablest spokesmen. Writing in 1923, J. Gresham Machen insisted that:

. . . liberalism has lost sight of the very centre and core of the Christian teaching. In the Christian view of God as set forth in the Bible, there are many elements. But one attribute is absolutely necessary in order to render intelligible all the rest. That attribute is the awful transcendence of God. From the beginning to the end the

Bible is concerned to set forth the awful gulf that separates the creature from the Creator. It is true, indeed, that according to the Bible God is immanent in the world. Not a sparrow falls to the ground without Him. But he is immanent in the world not because He is identified with the world, but because He is the free Creator and Upholder of it.[1]

Machen was not one to ignore theological differences of a rather specific sort, but he was able to sort out kinds and levels of disagreement, as can be seen in his observations about Roman Catholicism:

How great is the common heritage which unites the Roman Catholic Church, with its maintenance of the authority of Holy Scripture and with its acceptance of the great early creeds, to devout Protestants today! We would not indeed obscure the difference which divides us from Rome. The gulf is indeed profound. But profound as it is, it seems almost trifling compared to the abyss which stands between us and many ministers of our own Church.[2]

Why did *Christianity Today*'s editorial writer choose not to make the kind of distinction that Machen made? Why could he not have said that while some evangelicals would have "profound" differences with Hartford, these differences are nonetheless "trifling" when one compares the Hartford document with the views that it is criticizing? Is it that he disagrees with Machen that the question of transcendence is so fundamental that a clear affirmation on the subject is necessary before we can render intelligible all the rest of what we want to say? Or are there other factors operating that lead to *Christianity Today*'s negative reaction? In order to decide, it will be necessary to pursue some historical and terminological clarification.

Who Are the Evangelicals?

The term "evangelical," used as a theological label, is notoriously difficult to define precisely. To cut through some of these difficulties it should be noted that in using this term I mean to refer to a religious community that can be more accurately described as "American conservative-evangelicalism"—thereby allowing others to use the "evangelical" label while disclaiming one or both of my modifiers. Furthermore, I will not attempt to provide theologically necessary and/or sufficient conditions for identifying a conservative-evangelical; rather, I will point to some historical and sociological links that make it possible to discern a roughly identifiable community on the American religious scene.

The American conservative-evangelical community, as I see it, is a coalition of three subgroups. The contours of the first two groups have been noted in a number of helpful studies,[3] so that we need to give only sketchy characterizations here. The first subgroup, *fundamentalism*, began to take on a definite shape around the turn of this century, with the publication of a series of articles under the general title *The Fundamentals* —although the movement can be traced back further to nineteenth-century opposition to Darwinism, popular revivalism, and the Niagara Bible Prophecy Conferences. Convinced that modernism was a direct assault on the historic Christian faith, the fundamentalists waged a battle whose immediate goal was the maintenance of control over the seminaries and leadership posts of the mainstream Protestant denominations. They lost, and by the mid-1930s most of them scattered into splinter groups and independent churches. The resultant negative theological and cultural emphases of fundamentalism were influenced by their bitter experiences of ecclesiastical defeat.

During a period that began around 1940, there emerged a second subgroup that attempted to distinguish itself from the older fundamentalism. This group, which came to be known as *neo-evangelicalism*, was critical of fundamentalism on at least three points. First point: they were concerned about the anti-intellectualism of the fundamentalists, who somehow found it easy to transform criticism of Darwinism into a wholesale rejection of the "worldly intellect." Second point: the neo-evangelicals rejected the otherworldliness of fundamentalism, along with, for example, the obsessive interest in "Bible prophecy" that encouraged the flight from cultural involvement. Third point: they sought to avoid the extreme ecclesiastical separatism of the fundamentalists. Since they viewed themselves as having been edged out of the mainstream by liberalism, fundamentalists became fearful of compromise of any sort, even on what seemed to others to be very minor points. The newer evangelical movement stressed cooperation and intelligent discussion of differences. In this respect, Billy Graham's insistence on the need for "cooperative evangelism" —which included having liberal churchmen offer prayers at his evangelistic meetings—was a radical departure from the older fundamentalism.

As described, neo-evangelicalism should be viewed by the larger Christian world as an admirable improvement on fundamentalism. As the leading voice of the neo-evangelical movement, *Christianity Today* has done an excellent job of educating a large number of Christians on literary, historical, theological, and political matters. Among the neo-evangelicals there is a large number of politicians, scholars, artists, and the like who pursue their vocations with great Christian sensitivity.

Nonetheless, there are three important qualifications that must be added to our description of neo-evangelicalism's departure from fundamentalism. The first is that, while the neo-evangelicals treated intellectual pursuits with intense seriousness, they have tended to stress apologetic concerns over more constructive efforts. Their theological discussions have often centered on the methodology and presuppositions proper to the theological enterprise. To a large degree this is true of evangelical involvement in other scholarly areas also, with the result that neo-evangelical thought has tended to concentrate on the "prolegomenon" stage of scholarship.

Second, the neo-evangelical approach to culture has had difficulty in shedding the political individualism and conservatism of the older fundamentalism. This, along with the previously mentioned stress on apologetic themes, has inhibited the development of a creative social ethic.

The third qualification, closely related to the first and second, is that while the neo-evangelicals have been more open to a level of cooperation and dialogue than was permitted within the confines of fundamentalism, the posture adopted in larger ecumenical contexts has usually been a decidedly negative one. Billy Graham has been open to a cooperation of sorts with liberal Protestantism—but with the understanding that the fundamentalist content of his messages is nonnegotiable. Similarly, neo-evangelical theologians have not shared the fundamentalist's aversion to discussing theology with liberals; but the theological positions held by many neo-evangelicals in such discussions are basically those that the fundamentalists would assume if they were willing to discuss them. Notably, the neo-evangelical theological posture has been dominated by a concern for exactitude in formulating a doctrine of biblical authority.

The third subgroup that must be taken into account, even though it is quite difficult to characterize with precision, we can call, for lack of a better term, *confessional evangelicalism.* George W. Dollar, a Bob Jones University professor, notes the role of this group during the fundamentalist-modernist controversy, in his *History of Fundamentalism:*

There were many men with Reformed doctrine, Orthodox convictions, and Conservative views who held tenaciously to the essential truths of Reformation Christianity. . . . These men appreciated the outcries of the Fundamentalists, but they were never a part of their protest. The former were more intellectual and more insistent on strict adherence to Reformation views, and had little interest in evangelism and eschatology. Orthodoxy resisted the demands of the Liberals, but their set of answers was different from that of the

Fundamentalists. They did their best to preserve the Reformed faith, while the Fundamentalists somewhat bypassed the Reformation and went farther back in their appeals to restore the apostolic principles and practices.[4]

Dollar is thinking here specifically of the Scottish Presbyterianism of the "Old Princeton" theology—of which Machen, who refused to be called a fundamentalist, was a representative —but one should also add the following: Dutch Calvinist immigrant groups who had been associated with secessionist movements in the Netherlands; German immigrants who came to North America to re-establish "true Lutheranism," forming ecclesiastical bodies like the Missouri Synod; Anabaptist communities, especially the various Mennonite groups; and Episcopalians with conscious ties to the evangelical wing of Anglicanism.

While it is difficult to generalize about the collection of groups that fall under this label, each of them professes loyalty to a European (or British) theological tradition, usually one closely identified with the Protestant Reformation. In addition, the acceptance of a body of confessional documents (creeds and catechisms) and a developed liturgical tradition are often present also. Consequently, the confessionalists have differed on important points from the conservative Protestantism that had been nurtured in North American soil: they often had different standards of piety—many confessionalists do not strongly condemn the use of tobacco and alcohol, common taboos among American evangelicals—but they may have had more rigid views on such things as Sabbath observance or tithing; European sensitivities often led them to be critical of American political and economic practices, including ones accepted by the rest of evangelicalism; they tended to have different views on the role of education in the Christian life (often stressing the need for maintaining a separate school system), a much stronger ecclesiology, a different work ethic, and so forth.

My own denomination, the Christian Reformed Church, provides us with a good example of confessionalism's relationship to the larger American evangelical community.[5] From its American beginnings in the second half of the nineteenth century until well into the twentieth century, this group of Dutch immigrants maintained a critical distance from both the liberal and conservative wings of American Protestantism—a position that was reinforced by the conviction that American life and thought, including its various religious manifestations (which were sometimes lumped together under the label "methodism") were undergirded by an unhealthy pragmatism.

One important influence on the American Dutch Calvinist community was the thought of Abraham Kuyper, church leader, philosopher-theologian, and founder of the Free University of Amsterdam, who served for a while as prime minister of the Netherlands. Kuyper stressed the idea that the kingdom of God is a present reality—although it will not be complete until the *eschaton*—which becomes manifest through Christian attempts to transform various spheres of cultural life such as educational institutions, families, the political arena, artistic endeavors. The community of the people of God is required to demonstrate the power of the kingdom in each of these areas; thus, the institutional church is only one manifestation of the presence of the kingdom.

Unlike American liberals, however, Kuyper insisted that these "kingdom activities" must be substantively and uniquely Christian in nature. Thus he stressed the need to establish Christian universities, Christian political parties, Christian art guilds. On the other hand, he differed from the fundamentalists in viewing cultural activity as a positive requirement for the Christian life.[6]

American "Kuyperians" found it difficult to identify with the cultural attitudes of either the liberals, who tended to make too close an identification between the kingdom of God and secular movements, or the fundamentalists, who totally divorced the kingdom from present cultural involvement by viewing it as a purely eschatological phenomenon. But there was a general tendency on the part of Dutch Calvinists and other confessional groups to identify with the other conservative Protestant movements on the American scene. When Christian Reformed, Missouri Synod, and Mennonite church members did listen to radio programs and read periodicals from beyond their own circles, they usually turned to *Moody Monthly, Christianity Today,* "The Old Fashioned Revival Hour," and "The Hour of Decision." When they decided to cooperate with other Christian groups it was usually for the purpose of evangelism and Bible distribution, where their closest allies were American evangelicals. Especially on the leadership level of these groups, there was probably little if any identification with the older fundamentalism. But by the time Billy Graham began to conduct major crusades, and when *Christianity Today* was established, the cooperation of Calvinists, Lutherans, Episcopalians, and Mennonites was a visible factor.

Changing Alignments

Apart from a few qualifications (the kind of distinction Richard Quebedeaux has recently made between "Separatist Fundamentalism" and "Open Fundamentalism"),[7] this threefold classification of evangelicals would have been fairly adequate a decade ago. But more recently a number of developments have occurred which make the contours of evangelicalism—even the rough ones sketched out here—more difficult to discern. What follows is one perspective on these developments and their impact.

First, both neo-evangelicals and confessionalists have felt the impact of two recent waves of pietism, as embodied in the "Jesus People" movement and the "charismatic renewal." The influence of these movements has tended to reinforce some of the characteristics of fundamentalism. As one example, *Christianity Today* gave considerable coverage to the "Jesus People" phenomenon. Its treatment of this movement was quite favorable, even though the "Jesus People" were in fact reviving some of the less noble features of the fundamentalist mentality—for example, the anti-intellectualism, otherworldliness, and separatism that the neo-evangelical movement had fought in an earlier decade. It is not difficult to surmise that the favorable greeting given to this movement was due to a lingering hostility toward mainstream Protestantism, against which the "Jesus People" were interpreted as reacting.

Second, some theological polarization has taken place among evangelicals in the past decade. This development can be illustrated with reference to two test cases. One has to do with the way in which evangelicals have assessed the European neo-orthodoxy associated with Karl Barth and Emil Brunner (among others). Some evangelicals have followed Cornelius van Til and Gordon Clark in viewing neo-orthodox theology as the older modernism in a new and more subtle disguise. Others, like Donald Bloesch, have come to view Barthian theology as not only an improvement on liberalism, but in many respects an improvement on American evangelical theology as well.

Another "signal" type case has been the current controversy in the Missouri Synod Lutheran denomination. *Christianity Today* has consistently, even adamantly, supported the Preus faction as over against the Missouri "moderates." But there are many evangelicals who see the Seminex group as engaged in a legitimate struggle against a biblical literalism and an ecclesiastical totalitarianism that are typical of the fundamentalist mentality.

The story can be put in a slightly different way. The neo-evangelicalism of the forties and fifties was a conscious reaction against the fundamentalism that had emerged from the struggles of the twenties and thirties. Many of neo-evangelicalism's leaders had been trained in fundamentalist institutions, and they saw their task as one of an evangelical reconstruction. This reconstruction was stimulated by some substantive disagreements with fundamentalism. But many of the disagreements were of a tactical sort, so that the basic thrust of neo-evangelicalism seemed to come to this: How can we give *something like* the fundamentalist message a better hearing on the American scene? There may be a version of this question that all evangelicals would subscribe to. But there are sharp disagreements over how much of the task of reconstruction that began in the forties remains to be done.

To understand these disagreements better it is necessary to introduce additional labels. Within both the neo-evangelical and confessional groups there seems at present to be a growing division between progressive and militant groups. Thus, the coalition between *Christianity Today* and the Preus faction of the Missouri Synod seems to be one between militant neo-evangelicals and militant confessionalists; whereas Fuller Seminary seems to be staffed by a collection of progressive neo-evangelicals and progressive confessionalists.

However, this new pair of distinctions raises some new puzzles, which can only be touched on here by raising two specific questions. First, how does a progressive neo-evangelical differ from a progressive confessional evangelical? The corresponding distinction, between militant neo-evangelicals and militant confessional evangelicals, can be given some clear content: both have some attitudinal and behavioral similarities to fundamentalism, but one camp is likely to talk about a "truly biblical Christianity" whereas the other will appeal to the Scriptures as interpreted by "true Lutheranism" or a "thoroughly Reformed perspective." On the progressive side, however, it must be admitted that the distinction is less clear: neo-evangelicals usually become "progressive" by moving in the direction of confessionalism.

The other question is even more involved: How do progressive confessionalist evangelicals differ from those in confessional traditions who do not consider themselves to be members of the conservative-evangelical community? What, finally, does the evangelical label come to? For many of us, it comes down to the fact that there are basic elements in the evangelical understanding of the Christian message and life style that we cherish and do not find adequately treated in nonevangelical Christian groups: the sense that Christianity is a *message* (although it is surely more than this) that must be verbally articulated to those who do not profess Jesus Christ as Lord; an emphasis on the need for a "personal relationship" with Jesus Christ as Savior and Lord of one's life; a set of basic *attitudes* toward the Holy Scriptures, which are typified by certain devotional patterns and regular references in Christian discussion to what "the Bible says." To be sure, each of these elements has been the occasion for misuse and distortion. But, as many of us see it, these risks are worth taking in the light of the potential strengths.

A third development in evangelicalism during the past decade—and surely the most visible one—has been the much publicized emergence of an evangelical "political consciousness." This development has introduced some new styles and tones to American political life: Evangelicals for McGovern, radical black evangelicalism, evangelical feminism, the *Post-American*, Evangelicals for Oppressed Peoples. Many of these "young evangelicals" (the title of Richard Quebedeaux's book which has become a quasi-official label) have turned to the confessional traditions to find theological resources for their political concerns. The Anabaptist tradition, with its call for a community of protest and witness, is by far the most popular one among them, as it has been transmitted through the writings of John Howard Yoder, Dale Brown, and Arthur Gish. However, Roman Catholic liberation theologies, along with the writings of the Berrigans and Dorothy Day, seem to be running a close second in influence. There is also some interest in Reformed and Lutheran thought and in the pacificism and feminism of nineteenth-century "holiness" groups.

The young politicized evangelicals do bring some unique emphases to Christian political discussion and action. Some of them are former members of secular radical movements who entered the evangelical ranks through a "personal conversion" experience. Others are evangelicals who became "radicalized" through involvement with civil rights and antiwar groups. They possess many of the marks of evangelical piety and doctrine, and yet they have been greeted warmly by the liberal Christian left.

Many confessional evangelicals have strong sympathies with the political concerns of the young evangelicals, although they are fearful of the signs of an ideological mentality. I will deal with some of these matters in more detail further on. Older neo-evangelicals have other fears, such as those expressed recently by Harold Lindsell, editor of *Christianity Today*, in a rather poignant essay that he wrote at the invitation of a "young evangelical" periodical.[8] Lindsell warned of an erosion of belief "that the Bible is the infallible Word of God," and he went on to plead for a recognition of the "good things in American life that should be retained even as there are things that need changing." Social action, he insisted, should not replace a desire to preach to "the lost," nor should it undermine the task of bringing about a "renaissance of evangelical theology." Noting that young evangelicals tend "to be soft on premarital sex, homosexuality, pornography, and foul language," he concluded with words of advice and admonition: "Read your Bible. Pray daily. Be filled with the Holy Spirit. And don't let the devil get the victory over you."

The young evangelical movement has the potential for making the evangelical community a more visible and acceptable presence in ecumenical discussion. But it could also be an occasion for division and dissent within the evangelical camp.

A Critique of Evangelicalism

This rather cumbersome overview of American conservative-evangelicalism should at least reveal the evangelical community to be a complex phenomenon, with diverse tensions and tendencies. Indeed, a majority of the themes criticized by the Hartford group are such that, for each of them there is some segment of evangelicalism that either affirms the view expressed, or comes dangerously close to doing so.

This contention can be supported by some very brief observations on each of the themes and their commentaries, as they relate to evangelicalism:

Theme 1: Many militant confessionalists absolutize the "thought structures" of their favorite Reformation traditions.

Theme 2: Many fundamentalists hold to the theme as stated.

Theme 3: There would be no evangelical support for the view that God is "humanity's noblest creation," but much evangelical piety tends toward a *virtual* reduction of "religious language" to "human experience"—for example: "You ask me how I know he lives? He lives within my heart!"

Theme 4: The tendency toward reversing "the imitation of Christ" is a thoroughly ecumenical one; evangelicals differ from others only in the particular "models of humanity" that tempt them.

Theme 5: One evangelical version of this theme would read: "All religions outside of Christianity and Judaism are equally invalid; the choice among them is not a matter of conviction about truth but only of personal preference or life style." This, too, "flattens diversities" and "fails to respect the integrity of other faiths."

Themes 6–8: Evangelicals, as we all know, often have a weak view of corporate sin. What is not always recognized is that many of them have a weak view of personal sin as well. Sin is often treated as a lack of peace of mind or of meaning; the corresponding notions of salvation, then, come perilously close to "human potential" strains, as can be seen in the "God loves you and has a wonderful plan for your life" approach to evangelism, and the widespread notion of worship as a "spiritual fuel-stop."

Theme 9: Anti-institutionalism is the common property of fundamentalists, radical evangelicals, and many neo-evangelicals. The right wing views the state, and even the institutional church, as necessary evils. The left wing views them as *un-necessary* evils.

Theme 10: The Hartford commentary explicitly makes the evangelical connection here.

Theme 11: Fundamentalists would agree with this senti-ment as stated, thereby denying the need for social action.

Theme 12: Most evangelicals would reject this theme, al-though "Bible prophecy" buffs might balk at the suggestion that any of God's "designs" for the future will "surprise" them.

Theme 13: Evangelicals tend toward a thorough perversion of this theme. Some have so identified "human fulfillment" with existence "beyond death" that they have promoted a sense of radical discontinuity between this life and the next. In doing so, of course, they arrive at a position that is formally similar to the one criticized by Hartford: they deny any mean-ingful relationship between present and future fulfillment.

Ecumenism and Suspicion

Earlier, we asked about the factors that were operating in *Christianity Today*'s negative reaction to Hartford. We now have a basis for offering some likely explanations.

Generally speaking, we should expect progressive confes-sional evangelicals, along with their closest progressive neo-evangelical cohorts, to be very sympathetic to the Hartford project. But little support should be expected from fundamen-talists, militant confessionalists, and militant neo-evangelicals. There are a number of reasons why this is the case.

First, militant evangelicals tend to view the kind of confron-tation presently occurring in the Missouri Synod as a paradig-matic "battle for the faith." In the 1920s many of them might have agreed with Machen that transcendence was the funda-mental issue; this was during a period when the battle was heating up, and many conservatives were still operating within the mainline Protestant structures. At that stage, appeals like Machen's—to the common ground that they shared with others, including Roman Catholics, against naturalism—were an important part of their case; namely, that *they*, the conservatives, were defending the basic foundations of the Christian tradition. After they lost the struggle for power, however, more rigid lines of division were drawn. The question of biblical authority became the basic issue; and this in turn became closely associated with the narrower issue of biblical inerrancy. Militant evangelicals today are convinced that *that* issue is the one that inevitably plants a denomination on the "slippery slope." The Hartford Appeal can only appear to them as an obscuring of the real battle lines.

Second, it is unlikely that many evangelicals appreciate the categories employed by the Hartford group. (It is significant, I think, that the two evangelicals who did participate in Hartford are "Kuyperian" Calvinists.) Hartford calls for "serious and sustained attacks on particular social . . . evils," "relentless criticism" of institutions, a Church that *"must* denounce oppressors." This is not the language of militant evangelicalism. While there is more overall openness toward social action among evangelicals today than there was a decade ago, one is likely to hear the weak claim that "there is no reason why we should not be involved in social action." The Lausanne Covenant speaks in terms of the conjunction: evangelism—and social action, too. Hartford speaks of an integrated mission of "liberation" and "healing."

Finally, if Hartford had issued a document that consistently employed the vocabulary and categories of evangelicalism, evangelicals might have been even more cautious in their praise. Evangelicals have learned to be suspicious—and with some good reason—of the orthodox tones of ecumenical documents. They have learned not to take the language of mainstream Christianity at face value; indeed, they come close to assuming that the better a document sounds, the more reason they have to be suspicious.

The suspicion with which evangelicals greet much that goes on in the larger Christian world should not be simply dismissed as an incurable defect. Their attitudes are often legitimate responses to the ways in which they are treated; evangelicalism *at its very worst* is usually not as bad as some common conceptions of it that float around the ecclesiastical world. Evangelicals possess strengths, gifts, and sensitivities that can enrich the current ecumenical dialogue. To the degree that any portion of evangelicalism, even fundamentalism, refuses to be a positive and creative presence in that dialogue, the ecumenical discussion is thereby impoverished. Nothing of what I have said here should be interpreted as a suggestion that anyone be "written off."

Along these lines, one further observation should be made, although it should be accepted as an extremely tentative one. In referring to the conservative evangelical community, we are dealing with a phenomenon that, as I have already noted, has been to a large degree nurtured on exclusively American soil. It is possible that the difficulties that exist between Hartford and American evangelicalism are cases in point for a more general factor bearing on the significance of Hartford. On my count, fifteen of the original eighteen signers of the Hartford Affirmation represent churches with strong ties to non-Anglo-American theological traditions: six Lutherans, five Roman Catholics, two Christian Reformed, two Orthodox. This leaves three signers representing Methodism, Congregationalism, and Presbyterianism. Further additions to the group only slightly alter the situation, for example, the addition of two or three Episcopalians.

As we all know by now, the Hartford group was not organized in accordance with any strict quota system. Nonetheless, it may be that the underrepresentation of the more assimilated groups—Methodists, Congregationalists (UCC), Baptists, Presbyterians, and a good portion of evangelicals—was due to the fact that Hartford represented an attitude toward the theological enterprise, one characterized by a sense of loyalty to a confessional tradition and a high regard for "dogmatic" discussion that does not sit well in an American context that stresses the experiential and the pragmatic. This does not mean that Avery Dulles was wrong in suggesting in a recent article[9] that Hartford was a rejection of the "two extremes" on the part of a group of "middle-of-the-road or liberal" Christians. But it may be that the "road" he refers to is one that travels through the midst of *all* of Christendom. In that context, much mainstream American Christianity might be viewed as being very susceptible to the cultivation of extremes.

The Meeting of Left and Right

A number of those who have defended the Hartford Appeal have insisted that Hartford was not addressing the left exclusively. Much of what I have already said provides evidence for this line of argument. In the remainder of my discussion I will argue, in a more systematic fashion, that the specific "errors" mentioned in the Appeal are instances of more general attitudes and outlooks relating to the theological enterprise, and that these features are characteristic of both extremes in contemporary American religious thought.

The first three characteristics were mentioned earlier, when it was pointed out that fundamentalism often exhibits the traits of *anti-intellectualism, otherworldliness,* and *ecclesiastical separatism.* It could also have been observed that these are recurring characteristics of the American evangelical community in general. Indeed, I want to suggest that they are features which threaten the broad American Christian community, and not merely its evangelical wing.

These similarities between the left and the right of American Christianity can be demonstrated by a two-step argument. First, with respect to these three features, there are strong similarities between the evangelical right and the evangelical left. Second, there are, in turn, similarities on these points which can be established between the evangelical left and the radical reformers of mainstream Christianity. It should be noted that I am not attempting to establish a kind of guilt-by-association argument. The two connections are meant to be illustrative.

To establish the first connection, let us compare the attitudes of the older fundamentalists with those of the newer "young evangelical" group. Fundamentalists tend to oversimplify complex issues by resorting to rhetoric and the use of clichés. Thus, the only important question for Christology is whether Jesus was "a Liar, a Lunatic or a Lord"; the question of biblical inerrancy comes down to a choice between "the whole Bible or a Bible full of holes." If the need for careful scholarly treatment of these issues is proposed, the responses will come in the form of a refusal to engage in a critical approach to their own enterprise. "I don't want exegesis, just give me Jesus." "The only school worth going to is the Holy Ghost school of the Bible!"

Many of the underlying attitudes of the fundamentalists can be found among radical evangelicals, although the latter have turned to different sources for their rhetoric. Thus the "orthopraxy" emphases of those who insist that all Christian activity must be directly related to "identifying with the poor and the oppressed" resembles the fundamentalist complaint: "How can we sit around *thinking* when every moment souls are passing into a Christ-less eternity?" Fundamentalists and radical evangelicals, each in their own way, disparage "head trips" and tend to encourage mindless activism.

Just as fundamentalists shun cultural involvement in the name of "no compromise" with the world, the young radical evangelicals often express scorn at the idea of working within the system. They are in agreement with fundamentalism that the present age is ruled by Satan—or as they would put it, by "demonic principalities and powers." Christians, in both fundamentalist and radical evangelical views, are called to be an alien "witnessing" presence in the midst of a thoroughly sinful

order. The primary emphasis in each case is on showing that
"Christians are different" by promoting their own versions of
"a radically Christian life style": one group shows this by refus-
ing to use alcohol or to attend Hollywood movies, while the
other does it by living in communes and insisting that "voting
is a liberal cop-out."

The relationship between this attitude of otherworldliness
and that of ecclesiastical separatism is an intimate one. There
is a direct connection between how a group views the world
and its attitudes toward others who profess Christianity. If the
lines between church and world are drawn in a rigid fashion,
the corresponding distinction between those who are in the
"true" church and those who wrongly claim to be Christians
will also be a rigid one. For fundamentalists, this means that
their attitude of "no compromise" with the world translates
into a similar attitude toward those who call themselves Christians but who set up the distinctions differently.

Some radical evangelicals are moving toward an equally
separatist mentality. Many of them have already abandoned
"established" churches in order to set up "house church" worship patterns. There is a growing tendency among some to view
patterns of "fellowship" along rigid ideological lines. And persons who raise questions concerning the appropriateness of the
common radical rhetoric are often accused of protecting
"vested interests." Should this trend continue, the fundamentalist habit of meeting serious questions with accusations concerning the motivations of the questioner will have been du-
plicated.

The second connection—between the evangelical left and
the radicalism of the larger Christian community—is not difficult to establish. Indeed, the development of fundamentalist
type characteristics among Catholic radicals has been noted by
James Hitchcock:

Catholic liberals before the Council [Vatican II] professed to object
to all forms of fanaticism. They regarded the methods of proselytiz-

ing often used in the Church as vulgar and inhumane—high-pressure tactics not commensurate with the spirit of the Gospel. They deplored the tendency to divide the world into "us" and "them," the saved and the damned, those with the truth and those who were ignorant. They questioned, in fact, the very idea of conversion, except for those who came forth voluntarily. Yet by the end of the decade many of these same reformers had been "radicalized," which meant that they now approved the spirit of fanaticism, that proselytizing was an essential, that the world was once again divided between "us" and "them," although the distinction was now basically political.[10]

Some of the common attitudes shared by radical evangelicals, Catholic radicals, and the liberal Protestant left are expressed in William Stringfellow's recent book, *An Ethic for Christians and Other Aliens in a Strange Land*. The prepublication advertising for this book included the mass mailing of a letter of praise from Daniel Berrigan. The book's dust jacket carries glowing endorsements by Malcolm Boyd and Rosemary Ruether, and the *Post-American* gave it a lengthy review which did not include a single negative comment.

Stringfellow identifies the United States (and Nazi Germany) with the city of Babylon in the Book of Revelation. In his view, the biblical picture of Babylon is a parable of the presence of the moral reality of death in the world; but in a special way the United States is a unique current embodiment of Babylonian "death."

Over against "Babylon," we have the presence of "Jerusalem," a collection of faithful individuals and groups who perceive the reality of death that surrounds them, and who are looking for ways to "sing the Lord's song in a strange land." This group, Stringfellow admits, is more difficult to find on the current scene, although it surely includes some prisoners, the "Post-Americans," and perhaps the charismatic renewal movement and some "house churches".

Whether secreted within the established churches or detached from them, there lives in America a confessing movement—dynamic and erratic, spontaneous and radical, audacious and immature, committed if not altogether coherent, ecumenically open and often experimental, visible here and there and now and then, but unsettled institutionally, most of all—enacting a fearful hope for human life in society.[11]

Stringfellow's case has the classic fundamentalist marks. It commends the erratic, the audacious, and the not altogether coherent. The evaluation of cultural forces beyond the "in group" is a completely negative one. In spite of Dr. Ruether's promise that Stringfellow's book offers "rigorous theological analysis," one searches in vain for the hermeneutical or exegetical basis for linking "Babylon" with the United States, or for any explanation of what kind of claim is being made in the insistence that the "American way" is, without qualification, one of death: how, for example, does it relate to empirical data? Does the establishment of one-way streets, school-crossing guards, fire inspections, or automobile safety standards count as relevant counterevidence?

There is no doubt in my mind that the apocalyptic pictures of Babylon and Jerusalem illuminate the present historical situation. But why are the lines drawn in such a stark fashion by Stringfellow and his fellow travelers? Suppose, rather, that we wanted to sing "This is my Father's world" with as much verve as we might on occasion sing "This world is not my home." Then we might be inclined to say that while there is a struggle going on between Babylon and Jerusalem, the historical concretizations of each are extremely difficult to identify. Indeed, we might operate on the assumption that there are strains of Babylon that get nurtured among the citizens of Jerusalem, just as there are often surprising hints of a Jerusalem influence that can be glimpsed in the policies and practices of the Babylonians. If this is the proper picture, then the lines cannot be drawn once and for all; they must be continually drawn and redrawn from a perspective characterized by self-criticism and cultural sensitivity.

Closely related to the three characteristics or tendencies we have been discussing is what Richard Hofstadter refers to as the "Manichaean" view of the historical process, whereby

. . . the issues of the actual world are . . . transformed into a spiritual Armageddon, an ultimate reality, in which any reference to day-by-day actualities has the character of an allegorical illustration, and not of the empirical evidence ordinary men offer for ordinary conclusions.[12]

Much current "consciousness raising" is in effect a process of converting to a Manichaean perspective, from which ordinary conversations come to be viewed as a confrontation among "the powers of the air." We ought to be sensitive to the cultural forces and minds that mold our language and attitudes. But an exclusive concentration on those factors leads to a kind of dehumanization seldom noted by contemporary radicals.

The proper caution here was shown by H. H. Rowley who, in 1944, rejected the identification of Hitler as *"the* anti-Christ" referred to in the Scriptures; but he noted a "sound instinct" underlying such attempts to understand historical events in the light of scriptural archetypes—for, as he put it, "the demonic Beliar stands for a persistent force of evil, not in any one man alone, but behind all evil men, incarnate in them in varying degrees."[13] But at best this biblical imagery provides us, as do the radical theologies, with sensitivities and hunches that must be either borne out or rejected on the basis of scholarly analysis. Even if we had a direct revelation that, say, Henry Kissinger is *the* antichrist, we would not thereby have anything like an adequate explanation of recent American foreign policy. The same must be said of attempts to explain the Mayaguez incident by labeling it as American "imperialism" or "militarism." Nothing of this sort cancels out the need for what Hofstadter describes as "the empirical evidence ordinary men offer for ordinary conclusions."

A Testing of Hearts and Minds

Because of these and other similarities between the left and the right in American Christianity, we are often presented with false choices in theological dialogue. Fundamentalists view the Bible as consisting of a set of propositions that can be easily understood and must be accepted as literally true. Paul Van Buren, in *The Edges of Language,* offers the "educated Christian" an allegedly better view, one that recognizes that "our talk about the world is . . . richer than is dreamed of in the philosophy which defines religion as (incoherent) fact-centered theism."[14]

The problem is that by denying any fact-stating content at all in Christian discourse, Van Buren and his kind leave us with a view that in its own way is as barren as that of fundamentalism. If I utter the words, "the tree is falling" in an anxious voice while walking through a forest with my son, I am surely doing more than merely asserting a fact: I may be giving vent to fears, signifying my commitment to his well-being, or articulating expectations. But I am *at least* stating a fact, and any linguistic analysis that denied this would be an impoverished one because of it. The richer analysis here would take account of all the uses of language, including the fact-stating dimension. (However, we might want to avoid a commitment to too "rich" a view of language—many lovers' quarrels stem from too "rich" an interpretation of what one of the partners said. It is possible that many current interpretations of "God talk" are simply discourteous to the biblical writers.)

Another false choice that often confronts us is based on a commitment on both sides of the theological discussion to a naïve "What would Jesus do?" pattern of decision-making —although the extremes are opposed with respect to the "models" of Jesus which they attempt to impose upon us: for some members of the Fellowship of Christian Athletes, "following Jesus" means trying to win fairly; while for Harvey Cox it means identifying with the poor and oppressed.

Upon reflection it should be clear that the assumption that they share is an inadequate one. We know what Jesus might do if he were stranded on an island without a boat; we also know what he might say if he were asked if he was the Son of God. But it is not clear that we ought to imitate him in similar situations. The "imitation of Christ" theme as traditionally understood could avoid these ludicrous implications if it employed clear background theological criteria. But in current views, where Jesus is often identified with a select set of cultural aspirations, there are no built-in safeguards against a corrupted understanding of the person and work of Christ.

As a result, many corresponding prescriptions regarding the Church's proper mission are difficult to understand unless they are supplemented with some specific ideological content. Consider the proposal that we must (exclusively) identify with the needs of the poor and the oppressed. On most accounts of what this means that I have come across, I gather that radical Christians should have attempted to befriend Richard Nixon shortly after he resigned. Furthermore, this kind of compassionate action seems to comport with Jesus' pattern in dealing with Zacchaeuas. Yet most radical Christians would meet this suggestion with scorn.

I accept the view that a central concern of the Christian community should be to identify with the poor and oppressed. But it seems to me that we must get clearer about what that concern comes to by dealing carefully and critically with at least two questions. First, who are to be properly included in the class of the "poor and oppressed" with whom we are biblically compelled to identify? Are we to include Nixon, who is presently an outcast and a despised person? What about a financially well-off used car salesman who is experiencing a painful divorce? Or bored, pot-smoking students at an all-white suburban high school? Second, if we *can* clearly delineate the class of the poor and oppressed, then how shall we go about "identifying" with them? Is Mark Hatfield doing it? Will a professor who is properly aligned with the poor and oppressed inevitably oppose the construction of a new academic library? Will he or she refuse to buy works of art for personal enjoyment?

I am not clear about the correct answers to these questions; yet I am convinced that they must be asked and treated with critical care.

Professor Pannenberg rightly views the primary significance of the Hartford Appeal as residing in its "insistence that theological statements do not merely reflect personal preference but intend to be statements of truth, and are therefore subject to rational discourse."[15] In this, Hartford opens the way to the establishment of a climate in American religious discussion that many of us have been missing in recent years, one which permits us to avoid the false choices that have plagued us.

Of course, "rational discourse" can mean many things, and Pannenberg is also correct in pointing out that Hartford is not asking for "uncritical submission to what are viewed as the canons of scientific rationality." What we are pleading for is a climate of self-criticism and mutual correction that fulfills the Psalmist's prayer: "Search me, O God, and know my heart. Try me and know my thoughts! And see if there be any wicked way in me, and lead me in the way everlasting!" For the New Testament Church this divine scrutiny and correction is mediated through a community in which many diverse gifts are distributed. It is regrettable that many have not recognized the Hartford project as a significant attempt to promote such a communal spirit. But it is also encouraging that there have been so many—including many evangelicals—who have accepted the Appeal as a profound address to the American religious scene. If we succeed in opening up new lines of communication and new occasions for hope among this latter group, then we have made an important contribution toward building up the life and mission of the community of the people of God.

Notes

1. *Christianity and Liberalism* (Grand Rapids, Mich.: Eerdmans, reprinted 1972), pp. 62–63.

2. *Ibid.*, p. 52.

3. Cf. Donald Bloesch, *The Evangelical Renaissance* (Grand Rapids, Mich.: Eerdmans, 1973); Millard Erickson, *The New Evangelical Theology* (New York: Revell, 1968); Ronald Nash, *The New Evangelicalism* (Grand Rapids, Mich.: Zondervan, 1963).

4. *A History of Fundamentalism in America* (Greenville, South Carolina: Bob Jones University Press, 1973), p. 70.

5. Considerable information on this topic is included in Henry Zwaanstra, *Reformed Thought and Experience in a New World: A Study of the Christian Reformed Church and its American Environment 1890–1918* (Kampen, Netherlands: J. H. Kok, 1973).

6. An excellent statement of Kuyper's thought can be found in his 1898 Stone Lectures, published as *Lectures on Calvinism* (Grand Rapids, Mich.: Eerdmans, 1931).

7. *The Young Evangelicals* (New York: Harper and Row, 1974), cf. Chapter II.

8. "Think on These Things," *The Other Side* (March-April, 1975), pp. 17–21.

9. "Finding God and the Hartford Appeal," *America* (May 3, 1975), pp. 334–337.

10. *The Decline and Fall of Radical Catholicism* (Garden City, N.Y.: Doubleday Image Books, 1972), p. 38.

11. *An Ethic for Christians and Other Aliens in a Strange Land* (Waco, Texas: Word, 1973), p. 60.

12. *Anti-Intellectualism in American Life* (New York: Vintage, 1962), p. 135.

13. *The Relevance of Apocalyptic* (London: Lutterworth, 1944), pp. 157–158.

14. *The Edges of Language* (New York: Macmillan, 1972), p. 41.

15. "Breaking Ground for Renewed Faith," *Worldview* (June 1975), pp. 37–38.

That East and West
May Yet Meet

Alexander Schmemann

When the editors of this volume of reflections on Hartford
asked me to write a chapter on Orthodoxy, I was tempted to
decline the assignment, and for a very simple reason. It was
clear to me that the Hartford Appeal would not generate
among the Orthodox any significant reaction comparable to
the one it has already provoked among the Roman Catholics
and the Protestants. This proved to be true. Here and there a
few "triumphalist" remarks were made in which the document
was greeted as a welcome and timely sign of *their* (Western-
ers') recovery and return: recovery from what the Orthodox
always knew to be wrong, return to what they always knew to
be right.

But, on the whole, the statement itself, as well as the controversy it inaugurated within the American theological community, remained and is likely to remain extrinsic to the Orthodox
Church. The reason for this is clear: convinced that the trends,
ideas, and thoughtforms denounced at Hartford as "false and
debilitating" have had no impact on Orthodox theology, which
is true, the Orthodox see in the Hartford phenomenon a purely
Western development. While sincerely applauding it, they are

not involved with it and they bear no responsibility for the outcome. Hence, my first reaction was that whatever the future of Orthodoxy here or elsewhere might be, I did not see how I could relate it to Hartford or write an article about a nonexistent relationship.

On second thought, however, I realized I was wrong. I saw that this absence of reaction—or rather the reason for it—is in itself a very significant fact with implications, not only for Orthodoxy and its future, but also for the Hartford event and its own ultimate future. I realized finally that as one of only two Orthodox participants in the Hartford meeting I have a double duty: to try to explain to my Western brothers the true meaning of the Orthodox "silence," and to my fellow Orthodox why, in spite of its Western character and context, the Hartford Appeal concerns them, not less but perhaps even more than other American Christians. Such then is the double purpose of this essay, rooted in my own double and somewhat ambiguous experience: that of an Orthodox within the Hartford group, that of a "Hartford man" within the Orthodox Church.

A Question of Assignments

I said that the Orthodox reaction to Hartford—that is, its absence of reaction—is to be explained primarily by the Western origin and orientation of the Appeal. Because of this, the Orthodox do not consider that they have anything to do with it. It seems to me quite important to acknowledge the truth of at least the first of these affirmations—its Western origin. It is absolutely true that the Hartford Appeal is indeed a Western document, the term "Western" referring here not only to that particular—and clearly Western—religious situation from which the Appeal stems and at which it is aimed, but also to its basic theological presuppositions, conceptual language, and, in general, the entire spiritual tradition to which it unmistakably belongs.

While participating in the Hartford meeting, I could not help feeling within myself a certain inner *dedoublement*. On the one hand, having spent all my life in the West and having lived a quarter of a century in America, I had no difficulty in understanding what it was all about, in identifying myself with the concerns of the group, and, finally, in signing, in full conscience and conviction, the Appeal. Yet, on the other hand, as an Orthodox, I also very strongly felt a certain malaise, a kind of "inner distance" separating me from my non-Orthodox colleagues. Clearly there was nothing personal in it for seldom have I attended friendlier meetings. It was not a formal disagreement either, for, as I have said, I wholeheartedly shared the group's "negations" as well as its "affirmations." It was the experience, familiar to me since my first contacts with the ecumenical movement, of the Orthodox transplanted as it were into a spiritual and mental world radically different from his own; forced to use a theological language which, although he understands it, is not his language; and who, therefore, while agreeing on one level, experiences and realizes on another level the frustrating discrepancy between that formal agreement and the totality of the Orthodox *vision*.

If I begin by referring to that experience, it is because I am convinced that it would be useless to discuss the problem of Hartford and Orthodoxy without at first understanding the real meaning and the true scope of that discrepancy, and without realizing that it constitutes the main cause of that "failure" which characterizes the ecumenical encounter between Orthodoxy and the West—a failure which cannot be concealed by the massive presence of Orthodox officials at all ecumenical gatherings, and which is not less real and profound even if the majority of the Orthodox are unaware of it.

Thus, a few words about that failure are in order, and here again a personal recollection may be of some help. My own "ecumenical baptism" took place in 1948 at the first assembly of the World Council of Churches which was held in Amsterdam. And I remember very vividly how, upon my arrival and while going through the registration routine, I met a high ecumenical dignitary who in a very friendly fashion, obviously with the intention to please me, informed me that the Orthodox delegates would be seated at the extreme right of the assembly hall together with the representatives of the Western "high churches"—such as the Swedish Lutherans ("who, as you may know, *do* have the apostolic succession . . .") the Old Catholics, and the Polish Nationals. From sheer curiosity—for certainly I had nothing against sitting with those excellent people—I asked him who made that decision? His answer was that it simply reflected the "ecclesiological" makeup of the conference, one of whose main themes would be precisely the dichotomy of the "horizontal" and "vertical" ideas of the Church. And obviously the Orthodox belong (don't they?) to the "horizontal" type. To this I half jokingly remarked that in my studies of Orthodox theology I had never heard of such distinctions, and that without this information, had the choice been left to me, I might have selected a seat at the extreme "left" with the Quakers, whose emphasis on the Holy Spirit we Orthodox certainly share.

I hope that the point of this recollection is clear. The important fact of the Orthodox participation in the ecumenical movement and in the encounter—after so many centuries of almost total separation—between the Orthodox and the West is precisely that the Orthodox *were not given a choice;* that from the very beginning they were assigned, not only seats but a certain place, role, and function within the ecumenical movement. These "assignments" were based on Western theological and ecclesiological presuppositions and categories, and they reflected the purely Western origin of the ecumenical idea itself. We joined a movement, entered a debate, took part in a search whose basic terms of reference were already defined and taken for granted. Thus, even before we could realize it we were caught in the essentially Western dichotomies—Catholic *versus* Protestant, horizontal *versus* vertical, authority *versus* freedom, hierarchical *versus* congregational—and were made into representatives and bearers of attitudes and positions which we hardly recognized as ours and which were deeply alien to our tradition. All this, however, was due, not to any Machiavellian conspiracy or ill will, but precisely to the main and all-embracing Western presupposition that the Western experience, theological categories, and thought forms are universal and therefore constitute the self-evident framework and terms of reference for the entire ecumenical endeavor.

Hence the initial misunderstanding that has never been fully cleared, and hence the ultimate failure of that encounter in spite of the presence and efforts of many brilliant Orthodox theologians and spokesmen, and, in the last years, of the massive participation by virtually all Orthodox churches.[1] What the Western architects of the ecumenical movement never fully understood is that for the Orthodox the ecumenical encounter, first of all and above all, meant the first free and therefore truly meaningful encounter with the *West as a totality*, the West as the other "half" of the initially one Christian world, separated from Orthodoxy, not by a limited number of doctrinal disagreements but primarily by a deep difference in the fundamental Christian *vision* itself. It is this Western vision and experience, inasmuch as the Orthodox saw in them a deviation from and a mutilation of the once common faith and tradition, that they were anxious to discuss, believing such discussion to be the self-evident and essential condition for any further step.

Such, however, was not at all the Western presupposition. First of all, the West had long ago lost almost completely any awareness of being just the half of the initial *Christianitas*. Its own historical and theological "blooming" began at the time when the Christian East, which dominated the first Christian millennium, was entering its prolonged "dark age," was becoming voiceless and silent. Quite rapidly the West identified itself with *Christianitas*, the East slipping into a corner of its memory, mainly, alas, as the object of conversion to Rome or to Protestantism. Existentially, the West remembered, not its separation from the East but its own tragic fragmentation into Catholic and Protestant camps and the dialectics of Reformation and Counter Reformation. And it was then that, at first negatively and then positively, the ecumenical categories began to be elaborated and that the Western mind was shaped. Thus, shortly after World War I when Orthodoxy emerged on the ecumenical horizon, the shape of the Western mind was already there, clearly determined by Western self-sufficiency.

This does not mean that the Orthodox were not greeted with sincere joy and genuine Christian love. One can say that for a certain period they were even quite popular. On the one hand, their very presence—especially in the absence of Roman Catholicism in those early days—made the movement truly ecumenical and not merely pan-Protestant. On the other hand, these representatives of "ancient" and "venerable" churches were welcomed as suppliers of that "mysticism" and "spirituality," of those "rich" liturgical traditions which the West periodically requires as useful spiritual vitamins. There was, by all means, a "honeymoon." But to every serious student of the ecumenical movement it must be clear that at no time has the Orthodox "witness" (presented mainly, if not exclusively, in separate Orthodox statements attached to the minutes of all major ecumenical conferences) had any significant impact on the orientations and theological development of the movement itself.

The Needed Encounter

But how and why is all this related to Hartford in general, and to its eventual meaning for Orthodoxy in particular? My answer is that sooner or later, in a new way and in a different context, the Hartford debate is bound to face the same question that Orthodoxy tried unsuccessfully to raise within the ecumenical movement: the question about the spiritual destinies of the West, of that Western culture which has truly become today *the* culture. And if that question is not raised and faced, Hartford will, of necessity, lead to another spiritual dead end.

Indeed, the only consensus reached at Hartford concerns the alarming surrender of religion to culture, to the pervasive secularism of the modern world, and, as a consequence of that surrender, to the "loss of transcendence." But if that consensus is to become the starting point of a reconstruction, a re-thinking of our situation, then the next question concerns that culture itself or, more exactly, its own roots in the religion which today deplores "cultural captivity." It is precisely this question, however, that Orthodoxy addressed—although perhaps not very *claire et distincte*—to the Christian West; and it is this question that the West has neither heard nor understood.[2] It has not understood that beneath all divergences and disagreements, theological and nontheological, between the East and the West, there always existed the essential difference in the experience and understanding of *transcendence* itself, or rather of the essentially and uniquely Christian affirmation of both the absolute transcendence of God and of his *real presence*—that is, his immanence to the world and to man, to the totality of his creation. That which the Orthodox East rejected in the West, rather than clearly denounced, was ultimately the breakdown of that transcendence-immanence antinomy, of the basic cosmological, ecclesiological, and eschatological intuition of Christianity, an intuition which alone founds the Christian approach toward world, history, and culture.

This, and ultimately only this, stood at the heart of the debates and controversies which seem so hopelessly archaic and irrelevant to so many ecumenically minded people: the created *versus* the uncreated grace, the Palamite distinction between the divine essence and the divine energies, the essence of the mystical experience (the "nature" of the light *seen* and experienced by the saints), the essence of sanctification. None of these themes can, for obvious reasons, be elaborated here, and I can only declare and affirm that they are relevant and essential because they ultimately concern, not only religion and theology but precisely *culture,* as man's self-understanding and self-determination in relation to God, nature, history, and action.

What Orthodoxy implies is that virtually none of the "errors" denounced in the Hartford Appeal would have been possible without, first of all, a dislocation and a breakdown of the transcendence-immanence antinomy itself, of the fundamental Christian *theologia.* Just as all affirmations contained in the Appeal, which before being accepted and implemented must simply be *heard,* also imply and presuppose a radical reconversion to that vision. In a way, the Appeal sounds as if the cultural captivity and dissolution of religion, the loss by the latter of transcendence, were almost accidental, and that all it would take to improve the situation is a new balancing of our man-centered culture by a God-centered religion. Then, we are told, the Church will again be able to "address with clarity and courage the urgent tasks to which God calls it in the world." The whole point of the Orthodox argument, however, is that such balancing is impossible, would be abortive, without a radical re-examination of the process which, two thousand years after Incarnation and Pentecost, and after the call to *deification* addressed to man by Christ and the Holy Spirit, resulted in the triumph of man-centered culture and the secularistic rebellion against transcendence.

And it is at this point that the Orthodox question—aimed at the West since the very beginning of the separation— acquires its whole meaning. Thus, if the Orthodox are silent about the Hartford Appeal, it is not because of indifference or ignorance or some combination (typical, alas, of many Orthodox reactions to the West) of superiority and inferiority complexes. It is because *rebus sic standibus* they have nothing to say as long as the *preliminary* question, at which I tried to hint here, is not raised. Only then will Orthodoxy find its proper place in the debate on which ultimately depends the destinies of "modern man." Only then will Orthodoxy cease to be what it still is for the West today: a marginal supplier of valuable but unessential "mystical" and "liturgical" contributions, but which, when it comes to serious matters ("the task of the Church in the world"), is expected to express itself in a theological "idiom" whose very adequacy to that task Orthodoxy has always questioned.

In this sense Hartford may be a new beginning, may supply us with a new opportunity and new possibilities. The possibility, for example, of that genuine encounter which did *not* take place within the, by now aging, ecumenical movement. Such an encounter, as I hope I have shown, is needed for Hartford and that which it represents. But it is also, and badly, needed by Orthodoxy.

The Faces of Schizophrenia

I began this essay by affirming that the Orthodox nonreaction to the Hartford Appeal is rooted primarily in their conviction that the Orthodox Church was neither touched nor contaminated by the pervasive themes denounced at Hartford as false and debilitating. And in a way this is true. Orthodox theology, or better, the Orthodox confession of faith, remains not only conservative but, on a deeper level, entirely shaped by its essential dependence on the classical, patristic tradition. Thus, formally, the Orthodox can justify their *de facto* noninvolvement in Western theological debate.

But only "formally." For the paradox of the Orthodox situation is that it is precisely this theological conservatism, this adamant faithfulness, not only to the content but also to the very form of their doctrinal tradition, that conceals from the Orthodox their own, and I dare say tragic, surrender to that very "culture," from which they claim their Orthodox faith immunizes them. And the truly tragic aspect of that surrender is that they are unaware of it, naively ignorant of the ever-growing schizophrenia in which they live.[3]

There is no need to prove that today Orthodoxy is no longer confined to the East. The single most important fact in the history of Orthodoxy in this twentieth century is the growth of the Orthodox *diaspora*, the implantation of Orthodox communities in virtually all parts of the world. In America alone the Orthodox outnumber the Episcopalians and, what is more significant, their churches progressively lose their "immigrant" character and acquire those of the "native" religion. One of the signs of the irreversibility of this trend is the recent transformation of the former Russian Diocese, whose origins go back to Russian Alaska, into the Orthodox Church in America, an independent (autocephalous) church with no national or ethnic reference in its name. (It is still opposed, however, by many other Orthodox churches abroad.) Clearly, Orthodoxy is here to stay and to become an organic part of the Western religious landscape.

But—and it is here that what I termed schizophrenia begins —the Orthodox seem totally unaware of the tremendous spiritual implications and the challenge of that new situation. They do not seem to be aware of the fact that *culturally* the entire Orthodox Church (and not only the Orthodox *diaspora*) lives today in the West, exposed to the Western way of life and to the Western vision and experience of the world. They are naively convinced that as long as they perform their Byzantine liturgical services, and on each first Sunday of Lent ("The Triumph of Orthodoxy") solemnly proclaim their indefectible attachment to the "Faith of the Apostles, the Faith of the Fathers, the Faith that affirms the universe," they preserve Orthodoxy. And if, in addition to this, they cover the whole world with more or less successful replicas of Byzantine, Russian, Serbian, and other Orthodox churches; fight for the recognition of Orthodoxy as the fourth major faith; and remain attached to a few of their "ancient" and "colorful" customs, Orthodoxy is safe and they have fulfilled their duty. What they are not aware of is that the Byzantine liturgy—which they dutifully and in faithfulness to their Orthodox heritage attend

on Sunday—by its every word and rite challenges the culture
in which they live and which they enthusiastically adopt as
their "way of life" Monday through Saturday; that the Orthodox faith which they so proudly confess on the Sunday of
Orthodoxy contains and posits a vision of man, world, nature,
matter, entirely different from the one which in fact shapes not
only their lives but their mental and psychological makeup as
well.

Hence, the schizophrenia. The same priest who on Sunday
morning celebrates again and again the "epiphany" of that
Orthodox vision, will later—in the hall downstairs, in his coun-
seling, in his leadership—apply in fact all the "pervasive
themes" of the American civil religion. For all practical purposes the Orthodox have enthusiastically adopted the basic
principle of American religion: that it is very good to have
many religions (each one "enriching" the other with its own
"contributions," usually in the form of culinary recipes and
innocent, yet colorful customs) as long as deep down they are
in fact the same religion with the same basic hierarchy of
values. And since it is difficult to beat the Orthodox on the
level of customs and all kinds of exciting ancient ceremonies,
Orthodoxy enjoys a certain success and begins to attract more
and more those who, disenchanted or even disgusted with the
West, seek in things "oriental" the satisfaction of their religious emotions.

It is, then, this schizophrenia that, in my opinion at least,
makes or ought to make Hartford relevant for the Orthodox:
a question; a challenge addressed to them also; a mirror in
which, if they are honest, they should recognize themselves
and their own situation.

I know there are those Orthodox who affirm and preach that
the Orthodox can and must live in the West without any
"reference" to the Western culture except that of a total
negation, to live in fact as if the West did not exist, for it is
totally corrupt, heretical, and sick beyond repair. To achieve
this, one must create artificial islands of Greek or Russian or

any other Orthodox culture, shut all doors and windows, and cultivate the certitude of belonging to the sacred remnant. What these "super-Orthodox" do not know, of course, is that their attitude reflects precisely the ultimate surrender to that West which they abhor: that in their ideology Orthodoxy is being transformed for the first time into that which it has never been—a *sect*, which is by definition the refusal of the *catholic* vocation of the Church.

And there are those who maintain, as I have tried to say, a peaceful coexistence of Orthodoxy with a culture which, in reality, claims the whole man: his soul, his life, and his religion.

Both attitudes are ultimately self-destructive. Thus, what I mean by the "relevance" of Hartford for the Orthodox is contained in the question it addresses to us: if ours is, as we always claim, the *true faith*, has not the time come to show— to ourselves in the first place—how it works in life, in that eternal tension between the total, absolute, and truly apophatic transcendence of God and his real and wonderful presence in this created, fallen, and redeemed world?

Notes

1. Cf. my essay "Moment of Truth for Orthodoxy" in *Unity in Mid-Career: An Ecumenical Critique,* eds. Keith R. Bridston and Walter D. Wagoner (New York: Macmillan, 1963), pp. 47–56.

2. The reader who wants to understand the difficulties of the Eastern-Western encounter in the 20th century should read the essays of Father Georges Florovsky, who was for three decades the main Orthodox spokesman in the ecumenical movement. These essays were collected in three volumes: *Bible, Church, Tradition: An Eastern Orthodox View,* Nordland, 1972; *Christianity and Culture,* Nordland, 1974; and *Aspects of Church History,* Nordland, 1975.

3. Cf. my articles on "Problems of Orthodoxy in America," *St. Vladimir's Seminary Quarterly:* "The Canonical Problem," vol. 8, 2, 1964; "The Liturgical Problem," vol. 8, 4, 1964; and "The Spiritual Problem," vol. 9, 4, 1965.

Hartford and
Social Justice

Calling a Halt
to Retreat

RICHARD JOHN NEUHAUS

It seems unlikely that decades have moods. But people in time measured by time most certainly do. Thus it is said that the mood of the seventies is one of retreat; more specifically, that the churches are retreating from the commitment to social justice that motored the civil rights movement, the antiwar protest, and related crusades of the past fifteen years. It is not insignificant that the Hartford Appeal, issued January 1975, came at the precise midpoint of the decade. Hartford is an appeal to call a halt to retreat.

"Retreat" is, of course, a pejorative term. The more comfortable statement is that ours is a period for consolidating, for regrouping, for catching our breath. The implication is that the churches are suffering from an athletic orgy of overexertion in the struggle for social justice. The fact is that only a small portion of American Christianity was programmatically engaged in the movements that marked the tumultuous sixties. Clergy and Laity Concerned About Vietnam, for example, was for a time perhaps the largest antiwar organization and certainly the largest religious antiwar organization in the country. (The distinction is between a sustaining organization and the ad hoc mobilization committees responsible for some of the larger demonstrations.) Some of us involved in groups such as CALC were impressed by the thousands of clergy and lay people who rallied to the cause. Others of us, then and in retrospect, were painfully aware of how minuscule was the response in terms of the number of Christians and churches in America.

The measure of Christian social concern is not, of course, how many people are actively involved on "our side" of a particular issue. On the war, for instance, there were many who, equally motivated by Christian thought and piety, actively supported government policy. The chief problem in the churches, however, was not that of disagreement but of indifference. To be more precise, it was a determined indifference caused in large part by the fear of disagreement. It would seem impossible that a community such as the Christian Church, constitutionally committed to loving service to the neighbor, could stand aside from confrontations that meant life or death to millions. But so it was, and so it is.

How shall we explain this grotesque failure? Is it ignorance? hypocrisy? selfishness? hardheartedness? Coteries of activists on all sides of all issues are tempted to answer yes. "If only they were better people, if only they were really sincere in their Christianity, they would be with us." No doubt all the sins mentioned above, plus a long catalog of others, have a strong bearing on the unresponsiveness of Christians to the sufferings of others. But before we are too hard on the people God calls his own, we should at least entertain other explanations—explanations not so likely to confirm us in our several feelings of moral superiority, explanations not so likely to perpetuate the sterile polarities presently dividing the churches.

It may be, as Hartford says, that we are all acting on assumptions that are "undermining the Church's ability to address with clarity and courage the urgent tasks to which God calls it in the world." It may be that there are themes—latent heresies, as Avery Dulles argues in this volume—that are pervasive, false, and debilitating to Christian engagement in the quest for social justice.

It is important to begin with the pervasive aspect of these latent heresies. To acknowledge their pervasiveness requires a capacity for self-criticism. The more passionately we are engaged in the confrontation, the more likely we are to divide the world into children of light and children of darkness, and the less tolerant we are of questions about the lines along which the confrontation is drawn. For the Christian anticommunist crusader, as for the Christian revolutionary, the only question is: "Whose side are you on?" They both know whose side God is on. For the great majority of Christians the temptation is to seek God's will in a middle way that avoids readily recognized extremes. The suggestion that there is pervasive error is not welcomed by any of these Christians. For the first group, ideas that purport to challenge all sides are by definition on the other side. Such ideas smack of neutrality, and it is agreed on all sides of all barricades that, in the words of a former secretary of state, "neutrality is immoral." The battle having been joined, the measure of truth is utility. Whether the cause be freedom, as some say, or liberation, as others say (curious how one word capsules the great conflicts of our time), criticism that is not captive is suspect. And for the majority—captive to the polarities by which their middle way is defined—the suggestion of pervasive error is equally unwelcome, for it is easier to respond to other people's responses than to the questions confronting us all. It is easier to avoid extremes than to think and act one's way through to a new way.

A Place to Be Together

Hartford makes no claim to having discovered an Archimedean point from which all sides can be criticized in splendid isolation. Each participant in the Hartford group is both burdened and blessed by the social, cultural, economic, and political conditioning that variously shapes us all. Thus the Appeal does not propose a place where Christians can stand and move the world but a place where Christians can think and act together—and even, as we shall see, against one another—among the movements of the world. That *place* is the universe of prayer and discourse constructed by the truth claims of a transcendent reality; namely, that the whole of the world is awaiting the fulfillment signaled in Jesus of Nazareth who is the Christ.

Obviously, we are going to be getting rather theological. Surely, it might be objected, this is a waste of time. The best way to call a halt to retreat is to issue a call to advance. Maybe so, but that does not help us understand what brought about the retreat, nor how to avoid the next retreat, nor in what directions we ought to advance. We need not stop in order to reflect. The goal is to reflect in movement, and to reflect together while in diverse, even contradictory, movements. Admittedly, it is not easy. Many Christians do not believe in that universe of discourse that transcends all movements and universes of discourse—that is, they do not believe in the Church —and must therefore secure their parochial definition of Christian existence against all that might throw it into question. Others, impatient of reflection, would lead into the fray, becoming ever more judgmental of those who do not follow, ever more shrill in their loneliness, ever more conventional in their radicalisms, ever more captive to the intolerance that is the child of uncertainty. In rare instances, and in contradictory causes, they may offer the example of individual heroism— which is no little thing in a time as mediocre as ours—but for the most part they simply confirm their fellow Christians in the belief that retreat was the best thing after all, that social concern is for special people or special times, and not the vocation of us all until his kingdom comes.

The very term "social concern" is part of the problem. It suggests one item among others on the Christian agenda, one concern among many. All concern that is other-directed is by definition social. And "concern" is a feeble substitute for the more authentically Christian expression "love." Christian existence is a vocation to love. Loving service to the neighbor is not an optional activity for the Church. For Christians, the meaning of loving service cannot be explained apart from the love manifest in the Christ, a love that surpasses understanding, that is transcendent. To imply in any way that "an emphasis on God's transcendence is at least a hindrance to, and perhaps incompatible with, Christian social concern and action" (Theme 11) is to abandon the most elementary Christian assertion about the source and sustaining power of loving service to the neighbor. It is, of course, a possible position, it may even turn out to be a correct position, but it is not a Christian position.

Styles of social activism that suggest that the heart of Christian belief and piety is baggage to be dispensed with in order to be with the action will inevitably be, as they have been, rejected by most Christians. In a tactically similar way, if the struggle for justice is defined in terms that require hostility to the American experiment, forcing people to choose between the natural sentiments of patriotism on the one hand, and loving service to the poor on the other, loving service will be severely crippled. If the churches are to be renewed in their social concern, the call to renewal must affirm rather than deny the identities that are important to most American Christians. It may not be possible to pursue justice in accord with American identity and ideals. I think it is not only possible but imperative; but that is a question on which Christians can disagree. We cannot, as Christians, disagree on the infinitely greater importance of affirming Christian identity.

It is too easy to caricature the notions of religionless Christianity and of Christian atheism that have gained currency in recent years. At their best, the proponents of such notions wished to alert Christians, as it is always necessary to do, that the Church is for the world, that the promise of salvation is not merely that of individual salvation but of cosmic fulfillment.

The hope was that the "world" would no longer be a dirty word for Christians. The error was that the world was presented as the source of its own salvation. The goal of being a fully worldly person made it unnecessary, indeed a bother and embarrassment, to be a Christian. Or at least this was the impression gained by many Christians who listened to the exponents of religionless Christianity. Given the choice of being with the world (which presumably was synonymous with "God's action in the world") and maintaining the particularities of Christian identity, many shed themselves of Christian identity. Many more decided to persist with the bother and embarrassment of being Christian and turned off those social actionists who viewed that persistence as a sign of isolation from, if not hostility to, "what God is doing in the world."

"Who's interested any more in talking about God and prayer and theology when there is a revolution to be made?" That rhetorical question asked by the leader of a major Christian social action agency has been echoed many times over, creating a climate that reinforces the false and debilitating choice put to millions of Christians. Hartford says that it is "precisely because of" what we say about God, prayer, and hope beyond death that "Christians must participate fully in the struggle against oppressive and dehumanizing structures and their manifestations in racism, war, and economic exploitation" (Themes 11 and 13).

The downplaying or abandonment of Christian particularism and its truth claims was not, as some claimed, a bold leap of faith into the anguish and promise of the secular world. It may have been meant that way, but in reality it was a collapse of faith in the face of what was thought to be the superior weight of modern thought and its dogmas of secularism (Theme 1). In classical Christian thought, the world is a tortuously ambiguous reality. Christian truth claims are asserted *against* the world *for* the world. That is necessary because, according to Christian teaching, the world, deceived by the principalities and powers of the present time, is acting against its true self which is the future promised in the realization of God's final rule.

An Inescapable Embarrassment

This Christian assertion is inescapably an embarrassment because it is contingent upon what has not happened yet. The Absolute Future signaled in Jesus the Christ has not yet been consummated in historical fact. We walk by faith, when any sensible person would prefer to walk by sight. Our time and every time has offered various ways that claim to make it possible to walk by sight. Christians have always been tempted by these alternatives to our excruciating embarrassment. If they are true to the Gospel of the oncoming kingdom, Christians relate "to the idiom of [their] culture," learn from alternative ways of putting the world together, but say no to all allegedly final answers short of the final answer which is the coming of the kingdom. All other answers are "necessarily provisional." So important is this emphasis of Theme 1 that all the other themes, and a half dozen more that might have been added, can be seen as an explanation or midrash of it.

Christian claims are in inescapable tension with all other world views, ancient or modern. Any attempt prematurely to relieve that tension is to abandon the reason for being Christian. From Peter at the Council of Jerusalem, to Constantinianism, to the Grand Inquisitor, to Thomas Münzer, to the German Christians of the Hitler era, to Norman Vincent Peal and Juan Luis Segundo in our own time, cultural accommodation has offered welcome relief from that tension. It matters little that some of these figures are viewed as conservative and others as radical. The relief is as sweet and the accommodation as abject whether it be to forces of the left or of the right. All offer a way out of the relentless radicality that keeps every structure, thought form, program, or movement—present or projected—under judgment as "necessarily provisional."

The style of the accommodation, however, is not always the same. Those accommodations that are generally viewed as being to the left are often marked by greater candor. That is, the themes repudiated by the Hartford Appeal are more frequently articulated in their present or in a more muted form on the left than on the right. Indeed the insidiousness of culture religion of the right is that it characteristically appropriates the language of transcendence in order to hold off the transcendence that might bring it under judgment. The classic illustration here is the Grand Inquisitor in Dostoevsky's *The Brothers Karamazov.* Some who call themselves liberation theologians today frankly assert that Christian truths are only effectually true to the degree that they advance the theologians' favored revolutions. One is not as likely to hear a successful fundamentalist preacher assert that the Bible is to be taken seriously only when it conforms to the values, ambitions, and fears of his religious market. To be sure, one will occasionally hear it said that being a Christian is identical with being a middle-class, law abiding, patriotic American; but even in the circles where that is believed it is considered poor form to say it. Also, possibly, it is not said very often because such people have not thought about it very much. In any case, culture religion of the right is uninhibited in its use of the metaphors of transcendence, of God, of judgment, of life everlasting. But they are captive metaphors, neatly dovetailed with an agenda set by the world (Theme 10), apparently impotent in bringing that agenda under judgment. It is insidious. It is demonic.

Does that mean the metaphors are useless and should be discarded? No, it simply means the sacred is always vulnerable to evil, that the obverse of the holy is the demonic. As fellow Christians, we can only continue to make a nuisance of ourselves, insisting that we all be honest about the metaphors we affirm. If the culture religion of the left has the virtue of greater candor, the culture religion of the right has the greater hope of redeemability. Those who have bowed the knee to the revolution's false presence of the kingdom (Ellul) may yet, like the

prodigal son, discover their error and return. It may be, however, that they have abandoned so much of their Christian
identity, and so deliberately accommodated what remained,
that they have forgotten the way back. The fact that the more
vociferous protest to the Hartford Appeal was from those who
see themselves as left of center is a sign of hope. There was at
least a recognition of vulnerability to the questions posed.
Many who call themselves conservatives have been more
thoroughly blinded, as witness their widespread assumption
that the Hartford Appeal was directed not at them but at their
ideological opponents. Yet, no matter how obsequiously culture religion of the right bows the knee to Caesar, it still
worships a convicted criminal as Lord and God. Therein lies
its danger and therein lies its hope of keeping the metaphors
of transcendence in play.

We have spoken of culture religion of the right and of the
left. That can be misleading. It is adequate in speaking of
Juan Luis Segundo and Billy James Hargis and their sympa-
thizers, for example, because they themselves are readily
aligned with sociopolitical definitions of right and left. For
the great majority of Christians, values are not so ideologi-
cally defined as they are reflective of their placement, largely
class placement, in society. There are many worlds within the
world, and each has its agenda to which Christianity can be
and is accommodated. The radical church in Berkeley and
the conservative bastion of free enterprise on Main Street in
Muncie, Indiana, may both be victims of the loss of transcendence. Admittedly, if Christianity is to be in any sense a folk
religion, it must be "related to the idiom of the culture" in
an affirmative manner. But if it does not also critically confront that particular culture, it becomes indeed an exercise in
false consciousness and, no matter how it styles itself, is neither radical in calling to judgment nor conservative in preserving the troublesome fullness of the Gospel. Such a church
is but the pitiable victim of its own surrender and self-deception—a surrender and self-deception that, to the extent it is

blessed in the name of God, is compounded by blasphemy.

The retreat from social commitment that many see as a mark of the churches in the seventies cannot, then, be remedied merely by sounding the trumpet to advance. The reasons for the retreat—indeed for most Christians never having moved at all—call for careful examination. Hartford pointed to certain key assumptions that are debilitating to Christian mission, and I have tried to emphasize that these assumptions are pervasive, a point largely missed in the initial response to the Appeal. The issues posed by Hartford do not lend themselves to any "us" and "them" analysis along the lines of existing polarities within the churches. Indeed one purpose of Hartford is to call into question the way those lines have been drawn.

I understand Hartford to say that much that has passed for left or progressive Christianity demonstrates a loss of nerve equal to that which is perceived as right or conservative Christianity. The former surrenders with greater candor. It sees the culture, or a particular culture within the culture, as inherently attractive, probably triumphant, and therefore superior to any distinctively Christian definition of reality. What is called conservative Christianity, on the other hand, surrenders less consciously, accepting more or less uncritically the everyday values of the culture while isolating transcendent truth claims from troubling interaction with those who do not accept them, and from the sphere of social life in which those claims might call existing values into question. Both, however, remove the scandal and relieve the embarrassment of Christian existence. The alternative to this loss of transcendence is the persistent assertion, even celebration, of the tension between the Christian definition of reality and all possible worlds short of the kingdom of God.

No and Yes

The distinctively Christian witness on specific social issues will be characteristically negative. This is one aspect of our embarrassment. We hanker after positive programs that will carry the full weight of our, and God's, passion for justice. But the function of creative tension is to say of all that is and all that is proposed: "No, that is not the kingdom of God." Even the most attractive program is not "ultimately normative for the Church's mission in the world" (Theme 10). Our engagement in any program for change or preservation must be conditioned by the need to remain in the universe of discourse, prayer, and mutual criticism with other Christians. It is possible of course that we declare our opponents to be no longer Christians. That is an awesome judgment, however, and must be made, not on the basis of our confidence that our way is identical with the will of God, but only when it becomes manifest that the others are no longer even seeking to live in obedience to the revelation of God in Jesus the Christ.

Because Christians have said yes to the kingdom of God, they must say no to all exaggerated claims short of that kingdom. This is the Christian basis of what in other contexts has been described as "The Great Refusal." By speaking of the transcendent nature of that kingdom, we mean to say that it is, like God himself, Totally Other. We need to revive an understanding of the apophatic character of Christian existence, of the *via negativa*, of the way of unknowing. The transcendent cannot be fitted into any existing or conceivable scheme of things, need not be legitimated by appeal to anything that is or that we might make to be. Thus, "We worship God because God is to be worshiped" (Theme 8). Thus, in connection with social change, "God has his own designs which confront ours, surprising us with judgment and redemption" (Theme 12).

Yet Christians assert the meeting point between the Absolute Future and our everyday history in revelation most fully in the incarnation of God in Jesus of Nazareth. Of all our experience in history, it is about him and only about him that we can say, "Here is the kingdom of God." The Church witnesses to his abiding presence in the world as risen Lord, but the world is not yet subjected to him. He calls those who acknowledge him to join him in loving service to the world. Their loving service begins by calling the world to its true self in obedience to him, which, put negatively, means reminding the world (including ourselves) of its disobedience to his lordship.

The Great Refusal and the protest it entails is itself a crucial act of loving service. Were Christians simply to keep all institutions, revolutions, systems, and regimes under transcendent judgment, it would be a great service. Were Christian social action to consist in nothing but exposing and protesting all the barbarities and inhumanities that afflict our time and resist the coming of God's rule, our work would never be ended. Yet millions of Christians have become suspicious even of this creatively negative side of social action. They see churches, councils of churches and individual Christians protesting evil in a shamelessly dishonest manner that further exposes cultural captivity to ideologies, movements, and vested interests. The protest of social evil that is offered in the name of the Church is too often selective, informed less by a transcendent and universal hope than by tactical and strategic considerations. Bodies such as the World Council of Churches at least have the integrity to anguish over the difficulty of honestly saying no to all the forms by which the Gulag Archipelago threatens to encompass our century. Conservative opponents seem not to be even aware of the bondage which their self-servingly selected protests reveal. It is not only the minimizing of evil but also dishonest protest that "undermines serious and sustained attacks on particular social or individual evils" (Theme 7). If church members learn to distrust their leaders when they say no, they are not likely to follow them when they say yes to positive programs for change.

Christians must and do say yes to positive programs for change, not because such programs are the kingdom of God, or even the sure way to the kingdom of God, but because such programs offer possible opportunities for loving service in obedience to God and in the hope of his kingdom's coming. Positive social action is in response to human need. In this sense it is true that the world sets the agenda for the Church. The world, including the Church in the world, presents the needs. Christians have their "own perception of God's will for the world," however, by which those needs are defined and by which the form of Christian response is determined (Theme 10).

The Christian understanding of human nature, for example, should make Christians suspicious of complaints of oppression, victimization, or alienation which reflect, not human injustice, but inevitable and healthy discontent with a world short of its final destiny. Christians call the discontented to courage in this far from the best of all possible worlds. The Christian model of humanity is not that of complete self-fulfillment, which must remain illusory in an unfulfilled world, but the model of him who emptied himself in service to his sisters and brothers (Themes 4 and 6). Thus Christians resist the trivialization of evil that results from confusing injustice with discontent. Christian social action is love in search of justice. That is, it is the ongoing struggle for social relations and structures of greater fairness and moral excellence, as is appropriate to the dignity of those who have been loved as we have been loved in Christ.

Positive Christian engagement is unabashedly "for Christ's sake." Thus Christian social action is sustained by a relationship of command and obedience—that is, of discipleship. As Christians do not need the illusion that their actions are identical with God's will or essential to his kingdom's coming, so their engagement is not sustained by self-serving notions of personal liberation, by liberal sentiment about human solidarity, or by doubtful claims about preserving vested interests.

"We affirm that salvation cannot be found apart from God" (Theme 6). It may sound obvious, even banal, but it runs radically counter to pervasive assumptions in our culture. Social action as charity, with the patronizing implications that term has gathered, may, as they say, make one feel better or may even make one a better person. But it is not love in search of justice. Revolutionary engagement as consciousness raising and personal liberation no doubt has its satisfactions, but if this is its rationale, it is not "for Christ's sake." Nor are large numbers of Christians likely to be claimed for social action by the assertion that unless things are radically changed the poor of the world will rise up in revolutionary rage to take vengeance upon the rich. Most American Christians, who are among the rich of the world, have more confidence in their economic and military advantage than that.

Salvation, and the process of salvation, which is loving as we are loved, cannot be found apart from God. A "radicalized" Roman Catholic sister in Latin America protested as odious the notion that the poor should be loved for Christ's sake, as though they are not worth loving for themselves. But by what standard are they, or my next door neighbor for that matter, worth loving for themselves? It is simply a matter of sentiment or taste as to whether I view them as hindrance or help to my self-realization, thus justifying my desire either to eliminate them or use them. True, some astute philosophers and ethicists have contended for a factual basis to the idea that "no man is an island." But the average businessman and church elder is not likely, if he is the unsentimental sort, to be activated by the proposition that the things he values—his marriage, his second car, his spiritual well being—are threatened by the death of another starving child in Colombia. To him that child may well seem worthless. Indeed, as the proponents of triage, "lifeboat ethics," and other grotesqueries tell him, the child may be worth more to him dead than alive. There is no compelling argument to the contrary—unless it is God. Human solidarity is the foundation of love in search of justice. Human solidarity is not the given of which God is the highest symbolization. God, Creator and Redeemer of all, is the source of human solidarity. In its only italicized statement, Hartford asserts, *"We did not invent God; God invented us"* (Theme 3). Spelling out the meaning of that statement is crucial to the renewal of Christian social engagement in our time.

The Political Vocation

We have said that loving service is not an option for Christians; it is integral to human existence in response to God's revelation in Christ. But loving service may take many forms. Social action, narrowly conceived as political engagement aimed at structural change, is one form of loving service. It is an extremely important form that has been too much neglected by the great majority of Christians. Those who perceive its importance, however, have too frequently succumbed to the tyranny of the political that is such a prominent feature of modern thought. Thus it is said that all human questions are finally political questions and must be responded to through political action. As it is being advanced in some circles today, that proposition is false, and it is debilitating precisely to the social engagement we would encourage.

Political Man is one of the most pervasive of "contemporary models of humanity" (Theme 4). Psychological Man and Economic Man are among other powerful models. While speaking to each of these models, the transcendent humanity signaled in Jesus breaks the bonds of all of them. Social action as political action is undoubtedly the chief vocation of some in the Christian community. Were the community more open to the possibilities of loving service through political action, it would no doubt be the vocation of many more. But political engagement, in any commonly understood sense of that term, is not the vocation of the whole community.

With regard to social action, the most explicit guidelines

offered by the New Testament are those of Matthew 25. The giving of the glass of cold water and the visiting of the sick are, to those who are captive to the tyranny of politics, distressingly individualistic and apolitical. Matthew 25 is not easily related to such abstractions as defending western civilization or building the new man in the new society. It is not necessary, in order to sustain various forms of political vocation in our time, to contort the Scriptures into a manual for partisan action. Unfortunately, some Christians of all times have refused to recognize the diversity of gifts and diversity of vocations within the Church. Their form of loving service must be made *the* form of loving service. Thus they conduct forays into the New Testament discovering that the "real Jesus" is alternatively an American Babbitt, a guerilla fighter, a social reformer, or the archetype of the well-adjusted personality. The result is a loss of transcendence in which Jesus and his Gospel are packaged for sale in a market to be won for one's favored cause. "The danger is in the attempt to exploit the tradition without taking the tradition seriously" (Theme 4).

In our time there are opportunities for loving service which were not available to the early Christian community. It does seem possible to bring about far-reaching structural changes in political and economic systems, for example. But Christian social action aimed at these goals must always be monitored by the criteria of the concrete suggested in Matthew 25 and elsewhere in the Scriptures. Grand abstractions, such as defending the free world or making the revolution, must be kept under judgment in terms of what they mean for specific human beings and their communities. Some Christians, such as those absolutely committed to nonviolence, render an enormous service to all Christians in underscoring the urgency of the criteria of the concrete. That is, they insist upon a correspondence between means and ends that requires that they, in their vocation, exclude means which, on the face of it, contradict the end of loving service. Other Christians, perhaps more keenly aware of the twisted and provisional state of present reality, may understand loving service in terms of bombing Vietnamese villages or assassinating landlords who oppress Guatemalan peasants. Killing other people is at best always a very oblique form of loving service. But since most political programs of large scope at some point involve killing, either in their defense or in their advancement, it is the ultimate caution against absolutizing a particular course of political action. Politics, far from being the singular path to the kingdom, is under the sign of the Whore of Babylon. It is the vocation of some to take the risks of wresting good from an evil process, but they, like all Christians, act in reliance upon God's correcting and forgiving love. If their vocation is built upon the belief that their cause is God's cause, it is built upon sand, and it is likely to be very bloody sand at that. Again, loving service is the vocation of the whole Church; the political struggle is but one form of that vocation.

Hartford's emphasis upon transcendence has been criticized in some quarters because it precludes the possibility of building a partisan Church. The criticism is thoroughly justified. As I understand it, that is exactly what Hartford would preclude. The Appeal is, in that sense, catholic and comprehensive in its sensibilities. Transcendence relativizes every cause, movement, and thought form—most emphatically including those called Christian. It is true that God has revealed himself as a partisan God, but he has not revealed the details of his battle plan for the twentieth century. To be sure, his purposes are to be discovered along the fault lines of society, on the side of the poor, the despised, the outcast. But there is hardly a political option in the world that does not, with greater or lesser rhetorical emphasis, claim to advance the well-being of the poor. Individual Christians must make difficult decisions about these options, but they dare not demand that the Church conform to their decision.

We have seen that the ultimate caution in the political vocation is the use of violence. The ultimate test of whether this caution is observed is when Christians feel it their duty to kill other Christians. Is it blasphemy or is it an acknowledgement of transcendent mystery when two Christians come from opposite sides of the barricades, kneel together at the altar, grasp one another in brotherly solidarity, mutually ask for forgiveness, and then return to their task of killing one another? The illustration is obviously grotesque, and were its horror seen there would undoubtedly be less killing in the world. But it is not an imaginary dilemma.

There are two ways to avoid the dilemma. The first is to eschew the political task altogether, or at least to refuse absolutely to participate in violence or coercion. Throughout Christian history that way has been chosen by a minority, however imperfect must be its realization in fact. The second way is to apotheosize one's own cause, declare the opponent to be excommunicate, and thus bring into being a partisan Church. If my cause is "ultimately normative for the Church's mission in the world," then my conscience is relieved, the tension is relaxed, and I need no longer live in anxiety about unpleasant surprises. "Praise the Lord and pass the ammunition!" *"Gott mit Uns!"* "The work of the Holy Spirit in our time is the praxis of revolution." Clearly, as Hartford states, "This theme cuts across the political and ideological spectrum" (Theme 10). A partisan Church is the ultimate consequence of a loss of transcendence. It is the premature synthesis that is the essence of idolatry, it is settling for something less than the kingdom of God.

The political task—again, as that is ordinarily defined—must be seen as one vocation among many in the mission of the Church. On a tactical level, this seeming downgrading of politics will in fact, I believe, increase the plausibility of the political vocation for many Christians. That is, most Christians are rightly repulsed when told that the meaning of Christian existence is to be discovered predominately, or even exclusively, in effecting social change. They know that statement does not accord with their experience of all it means to be a Christian. It does not comprehend the mystery of communion with God, the knowledge of tragedy and redemption while holding the hand of a husband terminally ill, the awesome encounter with infinity in a snowflake, the ecstasy of great art that has no purpose but to glorify God in its very being, the devastating finality of one's own death. Many of these run-of-the-pew Christians, it is to be suspected, know more of "the depth of the riches and wisdom and knowledge of God" (Romans 11) than do their would-be teachers. When such Christians listen to those who say politics is what it is *all* about, they must think that they either do not mean what they say or that theirs is a very barren and truncated experience of what it means to be a Christian.

In calling Christians to social engagement, then, the tactical axiom is that less is more. To claim too much is to have one's claim discounted altogether. But more than tactics is involved. The very integrity of the Church's life requires that it not become "a noisy gong or clanging cymbal" vibrating to every cause, movement or fear that seeks to present itself as the Christian way. I have listened to a monumentally successful pastor from southern California explain that one source of his success is his studied avoidance of controversial social issues. "The people come to get away from all that." And I have listened to a pastor in another church declare as the Word of God that "Jesus wants every one of his disciples to be on that line next Saturday to close down the A&P." One is perhaps a sin of omission, the other of commission. Neither requires great prophetic courage, although the latter lays claim to prophetic courage. I find the first odious in principle and the second disturbing in implication. My hunch is that Jesus did want some of his disciples on that picket line. But on that particular Saturday, maybe Jesus also wanted at least one of his disciples to visit her old mother in the Bronx, and perhaps another to drive a truck so he could feed his children, and yet another just to stay home and pray for his niece going into the hospital on Monday.

No doubt I make too much of two very small incidents. But

by such small things the life of the Church is shaped; and by their cumulative effect good Christian people are confused, the Church's witness in the world is discredited, and we whimper about the mood of retreat that marks our present time. Both tactics and concern for Christian integrity require that politics be integrated into the whole of the mission of the Church, a mission which far surpasses even the most expansive human definition of politics. For beyond tactics and the integrity of a tradition is the core question of truth. Is it true what Christianity asserts about human nature, about the presence of God in our present, about the purposiveness of history, about the coming of the kingdom? Or must such truth, in order to be *really* true, become effectually true as measured by our social, political, or psychological agendas?

To Preach and to Pray

These questions are answered in large part by our attitude toward evangelism and the devotional life. Perhaps as much as any single factor, the divorce between evangelism and social action in the churches pinpoints what is currently wrong in our thinking about social action—and about evangelism. What frequently passes for evangelistic Christianity today reflects a massive loss of nerve, for it is afraid to call to a discipleship that —also in the political forum—challenges the structures and values of this present age. But our focus here is on what is wrong, and what might be done, about social action. We have discussed various ways in which Christian social action has made liberation captive to foreign agendas. I believe that captivity will not be ended without a major regaining of theological nerve. Thus, Theme 5 of Hartford, dealing with the relationship between Christianity and other religions (both "brand name" and secular), is the key to renewing social concern within the fullness of the Church's mission.

The widespread dichotomy between evangelism and social

action is unnatural and unnecessary. It is no more to be cred-
ited than the false positioning of the prophetic against the
priestly. Until that dichotomy is overcome, both social action
and evangelism will be crippled. Of course, as Theme 5 says,
Christianity must have a dialogical relationship to other ways
of putting the world together. But Christianity is proclamatory
as well as dialogical. As embarrassing as it may seem in a world
sated by the deceits of subjectivism, Christian claims present
themselves as objective and normative. Related to many cultural idioms, historically conditioned in ways beyond number,
seen through the prism of myriad world views, the Word
nonetheless goes out: Jesus Christ is Lord. To abandon that
Word and the mandate to proclaim it, is to lose all claim to
Christian identity. Christians proclaim it, not necessarily in
order to prevent other people from going to hell but because
they believe it is true, because they believe it is the most
important single thing to be said about human existence, and
because they are commanded to proclaim it. The failure to
proclaim that Word with clarity and courage is one of a part
with the capitulation to political agendas that are designed
either in indifference or in overt hostility to the lordship of
Christ. Among the young evangelicals there is today a serious
reappraisal of the connection between evangelism and social
responsibility, as described by Richard Mouw in this volume.
It is, sad to say, not as evident that the Christian procurers for
worldly relevance are prepared to rethink the meaning of evangelism.

The issue of truth is raised with at least equal force in our
attitude toward what might broadly be called the devotional
life, including everything from daily prayer and Bible reading
to mysticism and contemplative monasticism. Must these activities be legitimated by some prior social agenda? Might not
all these be forms of loving service, although apparently irrelevant to any present or conceivable program of action? To be
sure, the loving service suggested by biblical witness is not
esoteric but distressingly specific; feeding the hungry, freeing

the prisoner, seeing that the widow is not dealt with unjustly.
All these specific activities participate in the coming of the
kingdom, and our anticipation of the kingdom cannot be separated from them. But who is it that says the mystic's vision is
irrelevant to human need? Unbelievers say it, and too many
Christians supinely agree. People who say it have not themselves climbed the Seven Storey Mountain and returned to
report the effort futile. Christians recognize no measure by
which the search for God, the encounter in present time with
the Absolute Future, can be deemed either futile or useful. It
is the example *par excellence* of that which is an end in itself.
It neither requires nor can receive external legitimations. It is
therefore not enough to say, as some do, that such apparently
irrelevant activities as prayer and contemplation have a part in
consciousness raising for social engagement or in achieving
peace of mind to accept things as they are. Indeed such well-
intended apologies for prayer come close to blasphemy in suggesting that the search for God is in fact a search for some
lesser end.

But, it might be objected: Is not that the very meaning of
the incarnation? As blasphemous as it may sound, has not God
made himself instrumental to our human hopes? No, God has
indeed become vulnerable to human history, as is most cen-
trally evidenced in the cross, and calls us to join him in that
vulnerability. But if God is God, he cannot be instrumental to
any lesser end. That is, by definition, every legitimate human
hope is quite simply: God. By God we mean of course the
Absolute Future in the full realization of his rule over all things.
"Seek first the kingdom and all these things shall be added to
you." But to seek the kingdom in order to attain "all these
things" is not to seek the kingdom first. Unlike secular political
thought, which is totalist and truncating in its claims, Christian political thought reverences the myriad ways in which
God, and therefore our common weal, may be sought.

All Christians, then, have a vocation to loving service, but
not all Christians have a vocation to political action. To make

this more concrete, imagine a Christian who is an art historian. He happens to be on the spot when a child is playing in the street and oblivious to an oncoming truck. At great personal risk he rescues the child. Surely his is a commendable act of loving service. But now he is told that, if he really wishes to be a disciple, he has the opportunity to rescue—no doubt in less dramatic ways—people every day. He can be an organizer in programs designed to save the free world, or to overthrow multinational corporations, or to get relief to the victims of famine. Of course, if he cannot support himself as a full-time worker, he might have to continue as an art historian to pay the bills.

One hopes that such a person would resist the moralistic imperiousness of the above logic. One further hopes that those most concerned for the Church's role in society would support him in his resistance. "No," he might say. "I believe my study of twelfth-century iconography is my vocation from God, my form of loving service to God and man." When social action-ists recognize that the study of twelfth-century iconography may be as relevant—perhaps more relevant—to the coming of the kingdom of God as our next party caucus for whatever purpose, then Christian social action will be on a much firmer basis and have much broader appeal in the Church. When we stop living on nostalgia about mass mobilizations and recognize the minority status of the vocation to political change, we will be better able to respect the many forms assumed by the call to loving service. When we no longer contemptuously contrast the need for radical structural change with the individualistic and paternalistic deeds of love performed by Christians, one by one and two by two, when we learn to celebrate the small kindnesses which make the world a little less intolerable and that daily delight the angels, then perhaps we will receive a better hearing from brothers and sisters not so susceptible to political illusions as we tend to be. In short, the retreat from social action, if that is what it is, may end when social actionists are less arrogant, when they stop lusting for a partisan Church, when they recognize that it is the vocation of the Church to sustain many vocations.

A Public Faith

We have noted that the whole of the Hartford Appeal can be viewed as a midrash of its first theme dealing with Christian subservience to modern thought. While modern thought is of many parts, at this point in the argument I mean by modern thought those streams of post-Enlightenment thinking such as scientific positivism, empiricism, pragmatism, and others that have a determinedly secularizing thrust and have largely monopolized academically and politically respectable discourse in our society. For all the undoubted progress attributable to these modern world views, they have had a devastating impact upon the role of religion in society, an impact that, in its acceptance by many Christians, has transformed—I believe for the worse—Christian self-understanding. What passes for modern thought has largely robbed religious claims of their public potency. It has relegated religious truth to the realm of the private and subjective, and has established as dogma the notion that all assertions that cannot be empirically verified by conventional scientific method are at best irrelevant and, more likely, dangerous to public discourse.

Elsewhere I have written at length about the "sandbox of subjectivity" to which too many Christians have resigned themselves and, even worse, come to enjoy as a liberation from the obligations of rationality. We have mentioned the devastating effect of this upon evangelism. The effect is equally devastating upon the Church's role in society. In obedience to modern thought, many Christians have lost their confidence in the Church's right or ability to proclaim the Christian message in a way that makes a claim upon reasonable people. This is as true for those who have for all practical purposes given up on the evangelistic task as it is of those evangelists who urge the acceptance of the message "by faith" quite independent of, or even in opposition to, reason. Theme 2 of Hartford insists upon the social, that is, public, character of Christian truth. "The capitulation to the alleged primacy of modern thought takes two forms: one is the subordination of religious statements to the canons of scientific rationality; the other, equating reason with scientific rationality, would remove religious statements from the realm of reasonable discourse altogether." The first would appear to be the temptation of liberal Christianity, the second of conservative Christianity.

This same protest against a debilitating subjectivism is evident in Theme 6 and, as it relates specifically to social institutions, in Theme 9. If the notions repudiated by Hartford prevail, Christian influence in culture and society will continue to be pitiably enfeebled. That influence is largely dependent upon the claim that Christianity asserts a public hope, based upon public evidence, and subject to public discussion. Christianity is not simply a prescription that works for some people, helping them to be true to themselves or to realize their potential (Themes 6 and 7). Nor, as the conservative version would have it, is Christianity the offer of some spiritual salvation apart from the tasks of ordinary history. Only as we are seized by the public character of the Christian message will Christians have either the confidence or the right to insist that their claims be taken seriously in the public realm.

Many Christians who call themselves conservatives avoid the above problem by speaking of salvation in an antihistorical and spiritualized fashion that seems quite content to let the rest of the world go to hell (literally). Others, who *are* concerned for Christian social responsibility, spend themselves in trying to rally Christians to the support of whatever cause comes down the pike. Hartford has been seen by some as a reaction against faddism, and it no doubt is that in part. Hartford does not so much reflect weariness with fads, however, as it calls the Church to exercise greater discernment. It is probably inevitable that when a protest against a particular injustice gains a degree of popularity, the protest assumes some marks of being a fad. The fact that it may be fashionable in some circles to protest a particular evil does not discredit the protest. Christians should be suspicious of faddish protests, however, especially when, as is often the case, they emerge from the discontents of the well-to-do rather than from the real pains of the oppressed and powerless. It should be the natural instinct of Christians to examine protests critically and to throw into question the issues raised by movements and causes. They will only have the confidence to do that if they believe Christian truth claims participate in the same world of reason that ought to be decisive for the ordering of public affairs. Unless that confidence is discovered, it seems likely that Christians committed to social justice will go on serving up facile Christianizations of ideologies and causes of very dubious origin and intent. The Church will be viewed, as it often has been viewed, in terms of a great recruitment base. Organizations generically titled "Christians for X" will go on being second-level appendages to "Americans for X." And millions of people in the churches will continue to tune out the call to social engagement, in large part because they suspect they are being used and they do not like it.

Finally, Christian social commitment must be prepared for the long haul. Because so many were seduced by the illusions exposed in Theme 12 ("The struggle for a better humanity will bring about the Kingdom of God."), many of the radically committed of the sixties are today uncritical market analysts and computer programmers in the IBMs of America. "The revolution thing has been done." "We tried politics and learned it doesn't work." "I might as well rip off what I can for myself before the system collapses of its own weight." The illusions of definitiveness, and the emphasis upon personal liberation rather than justice for others have laid waste the commitments of yesterday.

Hartford points to a social struggle that is based in the Church's "own perception of God's will for the world"

(Theme 10). It takes institutions and the changing of them seriously (Theme 9), but it underscores the fact that all of them, most definitely including the Church, are "necessarily provisional" (Theme 1) and therefore dare not be confused with the kingdom of God. The Christian cannot be disillusioned by failure since he is not working by the metaphors of success but by the metaphors of discipleship. And ultimately the Christian cannot lose if Jesus is right and if his resurrection indeed signals the future of the whole human struggle (Theme 13). It is his abiding presence that sustains Christian commitment until that "if" is removed by the consummation to which he points.

The mood of the seventies, then, may be one of retreat from action for social justice. The Hartford Appeal calls for a halt to retreat and suggests new ways and new directions for the advance to be resumed. Whatever may be the present mood, the mandate for the seventies is that—with integrity, candor, high confidence, and unbending devotion to the truth—we stir up the gifts of the Spirit to sustain every Christian vocation of service in the world to which God has given himself in such great and reckless love. It is the mandate for the seventies, and for the eighties and for all the years that will be before his kingdom comes and his will is done on earth as it is in heaven.